THE PICK OF PUNCH

That's *SHELL* that was!

THE PICK OF
PUNCH

AN ANNUAL SELECTION

EDITED BY
NICOLAS BENTLEY

★

FOREWORD BY
MALCOLM MUGGERIDGE

ANDRE DEUTSCH

FIRST PUBLISHED 1956 BY ANDRE DEUTSCH LIMITED
12–14 CARLISLE STREET SOHO SQUARE LONDON WI
AND PRINTED IN GREAT BRITAIN BY EBENEZER BAYLIS
AND SON LIMITED WORCESTER AND LONDON

CONTENTS

CONTENTS

CONTENTS

Foreword

TREAD SOFTLY FOR YOU TREAD ON MY JOKES

I FIRST became acquainted with humour in the professional sense on January 1, 1953, when I moved across from the office of the *Daily Telegraph* in Fleet Street to Bouverie Street to become the eighth editor of *Punch*. It was, for me, a curious and rather sombre moment. There, looking across at me, I fancied with no great pleasure, was the austere countenance of Sir Owen Seaman, Bt.; out of the window I could see rolls of newsprint being hoisted into the *News of the World* for use that coming week-end. I had seldom looked at, and never much cared for, *Punch* as a publication, let alone contributed to it. Nor had I the faintest notion of how to set about editing it. A mood of doubt and despair settled upon me, intensified by the enormous and unfamiliar quiet in which I found myself. The pursuit of news is accompanied by perpetual and reassuring noise; humour, like love, must, it appeared, be sought silently, invisibly.

What is humour? I idly asked myself, and, like Pilate, did not wait for an answer. There is, I believe, a large literature on the subject, but I have never read any of it. All I have learnt is that what makes one man laugh makes another enraged; that the English, particularly, take their humour very seriously, and grow exceedingly angry at attempts to amuse them which they consider to have failed. It is not for nothing that, in the English language alone, to accuse someone of trying to be funny is highly abusive. Humour, I have come to realize, is practically the only thing about which the English are utterly serious. Like any other journalist I have long been accustomed to the unbridled insanity of the greater part of the letters addressed to daily newspapers, but these are as lucid as Voltaire, Gibbonesque in their urbanity, compared with the ones addressed to the editor of *Punch*. They rage and they storm, they insult and they abuse; they demand that the writer's subscription be cancelled, and avow that never under any circumstances, no, not even at the dentist's, will the accursed publication again be opened.

Nearly everyone I meet nowadays remarks that as a child he discovered the bound volumes of *Punch* in his father's library, and was enchanted by them. This picture of the tiny tot with a cumbersome tome open on a table, and the evening light coming in through a stained glass window, lost to nanny and forgetful of meal times as Leech, Tenniel, Du Maurier and Partridge were absorbed, is as standardized as the one of the French patriot who hid an R.A.F. pilot in a loft during the German occupation. I remember thinking, when such an episode was recounted to me for the, it seemed, millionth

time, that if they were all authentic the R.A.F. would have been so vastly more numerous than the Luftwaffe that the war would have been won almost before it began. In my own lower middle-class home there were no bound volumes of *Punch*, nor, for that matter, a nanny.

This omission I corrected (the bound volumes, I mean, not the nanny) by buying a set for £10, and thenceforth quite often turned over their pages. Alas, they provided me with no guidance as to how *Punch* should be conducted in the middle of the twentieth century. If the early numbers were harsher and more 'political', and the later ones more whimsical and 'conformist', no standard for the fabrication of humour was to be derived from them. I myself, as it happened, preferred the earlier, harsher note. Humour, for my taste, has to have an astringent flavour—like Shakespeare's Fools, who usually (for instance, the most splendid of all in *King Lear*) hurt in order to amuse, or *vice versa*.

Clearly, I decided, the business of a humorous or satirical magazine must be to ridicule the age in which we live, and particularly those set in authority over us. It is the gargoyle grinning beneath the steeple; it is Thersites mocking at pomposity, pretentiousness, self-importance and all the other occupational diseases of the mighty in their seats. Here a difficulty at once arose. The age in which we live is (as I daresay every age has seemed at the time) so overflowing with absurdity that it defies mockery. Who can parody *Hansard* or *Who's Who?*, or, for that matter, the *Congressional Record*? Where is the humorous genius capable of inventing anything inherently funnier than, say, the British Broadcasting Corporation, or, in its macabre way, the hydrogen bomb? What chance has comic invention with Earl Attlee, the Archbishop of Canterbury, Senator McCarthy, Sir Anthony Eden and Mr Khruschev about the place? When everything in *The Times* (except the fourth leader) is so hilariously funny, where is the place for *Punch*? Who will be bold enough to undertake to produce absurdities outdoing those which television screens, government press releases, City banquets, the House of Commons and Professor Toynbee constantly purvey? Try and invent a head of the Colonial Development Corporation more comical than Lord Reith, or a Minister of State who in the way of clowning outdoes Mr Nutting. It just cannot be done. The melancholia to which clowns, radio comedians, gag-writers, editors of *Punch*, and all who are in any way concerned in the humour industry, are notoriously susceptible, is due, I am confident, to being constantly confronted with this tragic dilemma of how to ridicule a world whose reality so often outdoes their wildest and most daring inventions.

I could provide many examples. Take, for instance, newspapers. How often in *Punch* we have tried to distil their vast daily outpouring of printed matter only to find our own efforts so much more sober, cogent and literate than the originals that we have blushed for them. I well remember the toil which went into a parody of the *Radio Times*, and how, when our version was finished, we were put to shame by an announcement in the current issue of a Third Programme talk on the place of the potato in English folk-lore.

The same difficulty arises in the case of sermons, political exhortations, Reith and other lectures, as well as votes of thanks, royal tours, the English-Speaking Union and Mr T. S. Eliot, not to mention the House of Lords, John Foster Dulles and the *Reader's Digest*. No one who has not tried can form any conception of how truly appallingly difficult it is to find anything in the world serious enough to be ridiculed. Before the visit of Mr Khruschev and Marshal Bulganin to this country we drew up what we fondly hoped would be a humorous itinerary for them. Imagine our consternation when, at the last moment, we had to delete a good proportion of it because it coincided with their actual itinerary.

And if ever we do succeed in achieving a valid and adequately barbed comment on the contemporary scene it is pretty well certain that we shall thereby lay ourselves open to the charge of having been guilty of execrable taste. Truth itself, I have come to feel, is in decidedly bad taste—which, from the point of view of an editor of *Punch*, is a most unfortunate state of affairs, since humour only exists in so far as it is truthful. The moment it departs from truth it is automatically transubstantiated into some *ersatz* product like whimsy. Mr Punch, with his crooked back and enormous nose and minute stature, is no respecter of persons. He has a naturally cantankerous disposition, with a natural propensity towards disrespect rather than consideration, towards criticism rather than acquiescence. His uncomfortable disposition makes it difficult, if not impossible, for him to be on good terms with authority. He has never appeared in an honours' list, never been to a good school (not even Haileybury), never changed for dinner, never shot grouse or otherwise disported himself among his betters. He is, in fact, decidedly non-U, if not a bit of a guttersnipe.

What is somewhat alarming, if one happens to be responsible for the activities of this deplorable individual, is to observe that the degree of public tolerance accorded him shows a marked tendency to shrink. For instance, in old volumes of *Punch* it is quite common to find the royal family being made the subject of highly satirical comment. Who would venture to do such a thing to-day? I doubt very much whether anyone would care nowadays

to publish an equivalent of so recent a venture in this field as Sir Max Beerbohm's admirable caricature of King Edward VII. And even such transitory and vulnerable figures as prime ministers, I have found, are liable to be regarded as in certain respects sacrosanct. Making them look foolish (no very difficult task) can evoke violent protests.

No doubt it is all part of a larger trend towards a collectivist, conformist society, in which humour (except in its meanest aspects) is repugnant, and ultimately has no place. Any orthodoxy protects itself, if it can, by making unorthodoxy a crime—whether against the state, or against the canons of good taste. To laugh is to criticize; to recognize that no human institution is other than imperfect, and no human authority other than derisory. Humour, that is to say, is a kind of resistance movement, which is sometimes indulgently tolerated, sometimes barely tolerated, and sometimes not tolerated at all. It all depends on the degree of certainty with which current beliefs are held, and the degree of stability with which current institutions are credited. A decrepit society shuns humour as a decrepit individual shuns draughts.

In a healthy, civilized society, it seems to me, everyone and everything should be open to ridicule. Indeed, I would go further and contend that the degree of health and civilization in any given society bears a direct relation to the degree to which this principle operates. Taboos, where humour is concerned, are an admission of doubt, and derive from a sense of weakness and insecurity. I have found, for instance, that the truly religious take no offence when attention is drawn to the absurdity necessarily inherent in the dogmas to which they subscribe and the ceremonies in which they participate. Protests invariably come from the conventionally religious; from the formalists for whom the dogmas and the ceremonies constitute the whole content of their faith. It is the same with politicians. Those who most object to being ridiculed have least confidence in the policies they advocate. It is the same with moralists. If they complain that some cherished principle is blasphemed by the humorous treatment of its application, then it is certain that in their hearts they doubt the principle's ultimate validity.

It is this very universality of humour which makes it so sweet an alleviation of life's bitterness. *Cette vie qui est si pénible et si belle*—surely an important element is translated from the category of what is painful to the other, of what is beautiful, by the faculty of laughter. As long as we can laugh—at our aspirations as at our disillusionments, at our fears and our pretensions and our vanities and our appetites; above all, at ourselves—there is still hope for us, and for the things we hold dear. Let us, then, laugh.

MALCOLM MUGGERIDGE

Looking Back

PROGRESS cannot be made up into neat twelve-month packages, and this year will perhaps be remembered more than any other year as one of unfinished business. The famous May traffic jam between Cannon Street and Pall Mall was given up as a bad job in July and the new road surface was built over it in September, but there is as yet no settlement on the question of compensation for the owners of the embalmed vehicles or for ground-floor tenants along the route, and we still await the promised re-styling of the still visible tops of buses, though their interiors are in full swing as underground conveniences. Similarly, though there was much talk of legislation to make the non-suppression of electrical appliances a capital offence, no Bill was introduced, and thirty million viewers continue to suffer from interference neurosis. Despite the passing of the latest plan, newly-built City office blocks have not yet been demolished. The findings of the Royal Commission on Vegetable Poisoning in Agriculture still hang fire.

Britain's armed forces have been fully engaged throughout the year, and during successive strikes and stoppages have moved in to operate the banking, tailoring and dry-cleaning industries, the Law Courts, the inland waterways, seaside deck-chairs, gamekeeping, cabaret, county cricket, upholstery and even religion—an anonymous Bombardier preaching strongly in St Paul's on Armistice Sunday. As a *quid pro quo* mutinies by national servicemen at Aldershot, Devonport and Cranwell led to a short but effective interregnum by Whitehall civilians.

With five deaths from heatstroke on November 5 and countryside ice-skating on August Bank Holiday the past twelve months have been of considerable meteorological interest. In February and March flooding in the North coincided with an official drought in the South, and emergency measures to transfer water from localities which had too much to those which had not enough were defeated by a sudden reversal of conditions. In April a Ministry of Weather was set up, and the Lord Mayor launched an appeal for those in stricken areas whose television sets had been affected by water.

The most sensational development in the Arts was the New Music, or 'Newsic', and thousands crowded the Royal Albert and Festival Halls to hear orchestras of a hundred giving concerts on hockey-sticks, bottles, kitchen utensils of every kind and tightly-stretched eiderdowns; M. Klangcz's concerto for steel helmet and rope-ladder fired all critics. More than six million people attended the lying-in-state of Ed Baloe, the panelist, after he had been torn to pieces by admirers while opening a fête at Pangbourne.

British sport benefited from the new barter system under which foreign racing motorists were exchanged for British footballers. There were teething troubles, as when an Arsenal centre-half and goalkeeper found themselves legally bound to open for the Gentlemen at Lord's, but all went well in the end. The year's most sensational attraction was the match between Wolverhampton Wanderers and an eleven of big Pools prizewinners (Wolves won, 270-0).

Abroad, the level of world unrest was well maintained. Oil dumping at sea continued. MM. Boulais, Trinon, Callé, Poussine, Propre, Foulard, Tricheton, Clambé and Montpoulet tied equal, in a public opinion poll, as the French Premier most likely to succeed. Russia claimed to have found the earliest known Chaucer manuscript, buried thirty feet under Red Square, and American fashion houses took up the vogue in one-piece, ears-to-ankle dinner pyjamas in radiation-proof tree bark. An invasion of Gibraltar by the Spanish was 'not recognized' by the British Foreign Office, and officially has not taken place.

All prophecies made, in Almanacks and other publications, about the events of this year proved to be false.

J. B. BOOTHROYD

Eric Burgin

Take Your Banana Skin Here

EVEN at this date you are, I'd say—looking over the candidates—fairly safe in putting down the name of C. Gordon Neill as the Year's Most Fascinating Statement Maker. Just in case anything has come up since and you, by this time, have forgotten C. Gordon Neill and his statement, and why it was fascinating, remember that he was the one who spoke about that motor race at Dundrod, County Antrim, where three motorists were incinerated.

There were people who were shocked, startled, even—as you possibly recall—critical. Somebody must have said—because the *Irish Press* reporter quoted C. G. N. as denying this allegation—that the future of the T.T. race might be 'jeopardized' by 'these events'.

C. Gordon Neill, in a position to know, because he is Secretary of the Six County Automobile Association, told the *Irish Press* that 'We could reasonably expect a bigger entry next year, and a bigger attendance—accidents encourage the public to come. All day hundreds of people drove from Belfast to the course to see the scene of the crash.

'The future of the race seems assured.'

It is a grand thing to have that stated: but where a lot of people went wrong was in not grasping the full significance and beauty of what the C. Gordon Neill Society, when formed, will term 'The C. Gordon Neill Idea'. Unfortunately the enunciator did not, in the circumstances, have time to get out full statistics: Would, for example, four, rather than three, fatal accidents have raised public interest in a corresponding ratio? Or does public interest in public carnage tend to tail off after a bit—in the sense that there are, for example, almost always an extra two thousand or so drowned in hurricane-flood disaster who came at the end of it and might almost as well have been saved for any effect they had on public interest and newspaper circulations? One hopes this will be looked into—nobody wants people to rush about getting killed and then, after all, no one turns out from, so to speak, Belfast to see the scene of the crash. After all, a chap likes to know.

What is little known is the fact—I doubt whether the great Neill is fully apprised of it—that for years and years a small band of people who realize the essential 'Neill Truth,' the truth that it's the slip-up that counts, has been working unobtrusively to use this realization for the public weal. As long ago as

1916 there was a man in the War Office who said the Battle of Passchendaele was going to be a terrible mistake. And the other man, who understood about accidents, said didn't this other fellow see that a big miscalculation like that about mud, and how many guns the enemy had, resulting in enormous casualties, was going to arouse public interest in war and the conduct of war to hitherto unimagined heights? He was right, of course, and his opposite number in Germany took the proper steps too, a bit later, and for years after that the people from—spiritually—Belfast dashed into the circulating libraries to read all about it, and you got Erich Remarque and so on.

I merely give credit for this incident where credit is due, because some of these pioneers of 'accidentism' in World War I tend to get forgotten, as men look back on the possibly even more vivid Accidentists of World War II.

One has no desire to single out any individual for special praise in connection with what was so essentially a team job, but it has to be admitted that hardly anyone in Britain would have noticed the German invasion of Norway had it not been for Mr Chamberlain's fine bit of 'slip-up' when he told the House of Commons that although the Germans claimed to be in Narvik, our experts thought they probably meant Larvik, because Narvik was too far up for them to have reached yet. The statement in itself was, of course, somewhat boring until the fact emerged that Narvik was where the enemy had got to, not Larvik at all. That drew the interest of the public at once, made people laugh at the Government, and keep an eye open to see what amusing games it would get up to next.

(In sincere tribute to the British Government's grasp of the 'untoward incident' as a means of packing in the crowds, the Russian and American Governments quickly followed suit. Nothing entertained and fixed the keen attention of the Russian public more than the realization that it had been a bit of an error to think the Germans were as nice as they looked. As for Pearl Harbour, well might any Washington politician have proclaimed that as a result of that little bash-up 'the future of the race seems assured'.)

Although often criticized for stuffiness, the B.B.C., in point of fact, has all along tacitly grasped the fact that 98 per cent of the population only listen to radio or look at TV in the hope of (a) an unscripted oath, (b) a technical hitch, (c) a girl's clothes starting to slip off . . . And this is where some of the new competitors are making a grave psychological mistake. To read some of the publicity material they circulate you would think they were going to put out programmes of faultless precision, everything ticking over like Chicago, and look what private enterprise can do compared to the bumbling old Civil Service.

A very poor approach to the public, one must say. More news of probable crashes, disasters, breakdowns, power failures, stars quarrelling publicly about their salaries, announcers getting all the names wrong, a weather expert on TV commenting on the drought in the midst of the year's worst rainstorm—that's what the customers want, and the Belfast chaps have proved it.

Come round down to it, who in this generation ever heard of the Foreign Office or wanted to get into it until there was the talk about Burgess and Maclean: since when the applications for entry from Cambridge alone have risen by nearly 21 per cent? Same thing about finance—you go coasting along without a crash or disaster for years and pretty soon you find half the customers have forgotten how to spell convertibility. Hardly a way to assure the future of the race. On the other hand, just announce to Reuter's one evening that all Britain's principal overseas investments have perished in a financial inferno, and you will have half the population dashing out to look. Accidents will have encouraged them to come. It is even deemed possible by some that a big financial scandal on the scale of the old Marconi Affair might get people visiting, once again, the Liberal Party.

CLAUD COCKBURN

ROY DAVIS

'*But that's stealing, darling.*'

'Oh dear! When they talk quickly I can't understand a word.'

THE CRYSTAL PALACE

To IT, three or four times a year, we are invited. Buses wind up the hill by devious routes, cars bump and honk, shivering motor-bikes start forward, people crawl; up, up, till over the skyline a pub rises —two pubs!—three!—and about this well-refreshed crossways there's a look that says 'Here you are!'

But where? One looks round. With the Palace gone—no glassy altitudes catching the sun, not a charred tower left—the sky, the whole neighbourhood seem vacant. I walk past a skeleton station (does it still house a skeleton train service?), past a fringe of sweet and fish shops, to the parade broad as a seafront.

London to the left, country to the right: there should be a view, but somehow it's got muddled. The wind plays with the few persons out walking, chairing one, inflating another, and causing a dog to travel more slantwise than usual. A nursemaid jaunts a pram, and a man looks up from his newspaper to catch smiles; she won't have it; turned down by the

16

world he returns to the news of it; bells sound, milk bottles chink . . . These are the doings of Sydenham.

Across the way the crowd, the urban crowd to which properly I belong, thrusts on along a high black fence encompassing—nothing. A holiday listlessness possesses many, but there are hurriers. I join them. We are looking for a way in. Every arrow and finger point back, but we must know what we are doing, and here are cars too, and motor-bikes, nosing.

And, sure enough, after a while we meet the drive-in, the crunch of cinders, armleted arms raised, turnstiles clicking.

'This Sport is DANGEROUS'—one reason why we're here. Why *am* I here? Oh, of course, motor-cycle racing. 'Dogs,' says another board, 'Not Admitted.' Seems hard. Where can a dog turn? Brushed off pavements, debarred from restaurants, opera; and only last week I noticed over a shiny-tiled doorway 'MEN—No Dogs'.

But there are one or two gay ones flaunting scarves, singing, playing leap-frog over the waste of what looks like old gun emplacements, and is, in fact, the very ground of the Crystal Palace.

Yes, here where I'm standing stood the last surviving tower, and there, a couple of hundred yards away, rose the other; and between the two on his tight-rope Blondin walked, pausing halfway to cook and eat an omelet. The occasion demanded no less. Here the choirs sang and the silversmiths danced and parrots screeched and there were orgies of Handel, and Gilbert and Sullivan, and here (on Thursday evenings) the fireworks gushed, and hot-gospellers cooled their

converts in tanks, and on a night most memorable the whole thing went up in flames, glass melted, iron twisted and sank—the end fabulous as the beginning.

But if the jewel is vanished, the setting remains. Grand terraces, a quarter of a mile wide, go down the hill in steps, and on each terrace are balustrades with figures. Those nearest seem to represent Empire—coolies, rubber planters, far-flung nurses, Sepoys, blacks, peerers over veld and peggers of gold—ah, those were the days!—the conqueror and the conquered whom Time, negligent elsewhere, has preserved here with smudged countenances and a hand or arm lost—no, fallen, it lies below, couched in weeds.

I walk on in sunlight, and on a broken pillar lifting into the blue are cut visitors' initials: it might be Carthage. But a little farther on, and back in history, I reach a courtyard posted by four lion-women. What secret they guarded, what rites and eventual ruin were theirs, who can tell?

The sun dazzles. Eternity broods. Then into this hollow, as in some storm-wracked shell held to the ear, comes a roar of machines. The races have started!

Two Martians leap out of nowhere—from behind one of the lion-women, I fancy, where they have been kissing—and waddle off to join the throng making its way down to the track. This curls a ribbon, visible in parts, round a woody hinterland below. There are others helmeted and space-suited, giving character to a crowd that might otherwise be after point-to-point or cricket. They pass Hermes and Queen Victoria, a pool in which bathe river gods, Thames, Dee, Avon; and where all now is reeds, once rose the fountains that out-topped Versailles. On down steps, with flowers bursting through cracks, across a terrace, past a disc-thrower who has dropped his disc and an urn toppled, cherubs with fig-leaves and blind sentinels, to a large central basin: over this the crowd pours, and two schoolgirls, with arms twined, discover Pan.

Now the din is terrific. It opens and shuts

as the dark shapes slant round a bend, disappear behind trees; then with a roar and a whine to make Mr Gladstone blink, they flick past. You never saw, or heard, such swank.

Swans on a lake seem deaf, and children play in a neglected band-stand.

My perch commands about one third of the course, and I sit with legs dangling at the feet of Dawn: I think it must be Dawn, from the lady's cringing modesty, or Early Dip; Nature has come to her rescue with a network of ivy over head and trunk and down one leg, giving her an air of outrageous chic.

There's a hallucination in the mad bikes whizzing round and round. One gets to know those with the more urgent note—the mosquito that will sting; then a lull, the reverberations die away, but loud-speakers continue to haunt the wood. Race with side-cars. On these a passenger lies prone like a sled rider, ready at the least deflection or curve to lean far out over the track or swing his weight on the pillion. A white ambulance stands by. I've no need of a programme,

the wood demon tells all; and I learn that what we've been witnessing are mere practice bouts, a warming up for the afternoon when the real thing will start, with stands filled, knolls covered, the track thickly lined, beer and ice-cream paddocks strewn.

Shall I stay? The announcement of a ninety-minute lunch interval clinches it. I walk on downhill.

Wonders never cease. Here's an avenue and an enormous head in granite frowning on me out of the trees: Sir Joseph Paxton himself, the author of our dilapidated pleasure.

Crowds are moving in by the bottom entrance, but I manage to fight my way out. 'You can't come back!' shouts an official. I shan't!

But one stupendous touch of fancy still waits. In the public park is a lake with islands and ducks and boats; and people are enjoying the idyll, no more disturbed by a brontosaurus (life size), shouldering its way out of water, pterodactyls, iguanodons and the like, than by the empty roar up the hill.

G. W. STONIER

'They've closed.'

The Residue

IMMORTALITY on this earth being, unaccountably, not yet available, it is a comfort to read an advertisement headed EFFICIENT PULVERIZATION OF RESIDUES. At least we can be well disposed of. The machine, designed by specialists in pulverizing equipment, combines happily Rapidity and Silent Operation with Freedom from Dust and Accessibility for Opening, Cleaning and Maintenance. It has Magnetic Separation, and needs only light bolting down. Above all it reduces Ashes to the Ideal Grade for Scattering. An Atomiser, with a 3 h.p. Squirrel Cage Motor with Starter and Isolation Switch, does likewise. These are among the civilized amenities offered

Funeral Service Journal. 'O what a wonderful evening!' they record, of a recent 'memorable ladies' festival' at a Park Lane Hotel, with 'hospitality and entertainment on a most generous scale'. The speeches were lively, notably that of Mr Turner. Describing himself as a 'bit of a lady killer', he reserved special praise for the lady guests: 'It is wonderful that they should come along and make this evening so adorable.' The cabaret consisted of speciality, acrobatic and chorus dancing at breath-taking speed, and there was only a single allusion to death, in suitably jocular terms, by an M.P., who had recently addressed a distinguished collection of doctors, and supposed

for sale in a quarterly named *Pharos*, the official journal of the Cremation Movement.

We shall be disposed of, moreover, by charming, respectable people. Undertakers no longer, they have attained on the contrary to the social status of Upholders, or more commonly Funeral Directors. And this is their gala year. Next week they will be in Blackpool, celebrating a 'glorious occasion'—the jubilee of the National Association of Funeral Directors. The highlight of the celebrations will be a funeral banquet, to which guests will fly, from London and Birmingham, in specially chartered aircraft. In ideal holiday weather they will enjoy a week of social events, with many attractions and entertainments, to say nothing of a conference, and an exhibition of funeral equipment throughout the ages.

These disposers of residue are sociable people, whose entertainments are recorded monthly in a

that 'speaking to an association of funeral directors could be described as logical progress'. (*Laughter*).

More fortunate than their clients, they are healthy people, for ever congratulating one another, in the pages of their journal, on complete recovery from serious illness. They are people of taste. 'There is no reason for our headquarters to be gloomy,' they say. Thus the new board room has paper in grey-and-white stripes on three walls, and vermilion with white stars, on the fourth, while the office of the 'bustling, cheerful secretary', Miss Hurry, is painted in cyclamen and primrose, with Regency brocade curtains.

They are humorous people. The rotund Mr Furphy, for a long time the only embalmer in Belfast, was once 'knighted' by the President of the Association, who, 'touching him on the head in traditional manner, said, "Arise, Circumference!"' Nor are they blind to the arts. Another noted embalmer, at a recent meeting in North Middlesex, favourably compared the art of funeral direction to the art of ballet. 'Ballet,' he said, 'is a bastard art in which an unsuccessful attempt has been made to wed motion and music . . . Undertaking is similar, though at a far greater disadvantage, inasmuch as it attempts to wed not two but many distinct skills, adequate knowledge of one of which should yield a better return in cash and status than this industry can give.'

This embalmer, a Mr Hall (M.B.I.E., M.B.E.S.), is a gentleman who, reassuringly, knows his job. Month after month he contributes to the journal a learned serial, under the title of 'Embalming Technique'. He recommends a pair of fine-nosed forceps which 'enable one . . . to pack the eyes, for example, with a delicacy of touch which the heavier patterns deny'. He urges one to 'avoid the common error of raising the femoral vessels low on the thigh'. He assumes that one knows, 'to paraphrase Macaulay (*sic*), that the axillary artery lies along the inner border of the coraco-brachialis muscle and immediately behind the median nerve'.

'Even a funeral director,' however, 'has his problems'. The Association lately had occasion to complain to British Railways of the way a coffin was handled. 'It was said that the coffin, without a covering, was put on a trolley and pushed along the platform the same way as baggage.' It might have contained any of us. Then there is 'the worry and difficulty of death abroad' now solved (for the funeral director) by an International Cremation Federation. Finally, he must always know 'where he can get his coffins and other requisites at the right price when demand is great'.

The advertisement columns offer an inviting array to choose from. There are coffins at various prices in English elm and oak, in Japanese elm and oak, in African agba, idigbo and obeche, even in plywood ('immense strength, light weight, good appearance'). Specialities are an Anglo-Yankee Shine or a super-wax polish ('gives a brilliant wax finish which does not finger-mark'). There is a 'completely combustible' coffin, in an 'entirely new material,' for cremation; there is another, plush-covered, in purple, maroon or grey. There are Shrouds, Sidesheets and Ruffles, in swansdown, calico and wadding. There is the 'dry ice' method of pre-burial sanitation.

So all will be well. A streamlined deck hearse will remove the residue, followed closely by limousines for the living. After an appropriate valedictory it will be transferred to 'a superheated retort', fired perhaps by gas ('unsurpassed for ease of control, smokeless

and clean in operation, economical') perhaps by electricity ('a compact and highly efficient unit, designed for convenience and utility'), in any case 'effecting in less than two hours a result which could only be accomplished after many years by burial'. The exact time taken will 'depend upon the build, weight and water content of the subject'. Following 'rapid oxidation of the body tissues' the subject's bones will be 'crushed to a fine ash by hand with a pestle and mortar or in a pulverizing machine'.

We are now a fine white ash, 'of greyish colour, and weighing some five pounds'. What is to be done with us? A bulkier residue might have rested, in eternal respectability, in Pine Avenue or Larch Avenue or Laurel Avenue or even The Crescent, amid the shrubberies and the 'stately Wellingtonias' of the London Necropolis, at peace but for the eternal roar of trains and the rattle of machine-gun fire from Bisley. But to-day (or so we are assured by the Headingley-cum-Burley Burial Board), 'a family accepting the cremation as the means of disposal of a loved one is no longer considered to be eccentric'. Hence the residue may be disposed of, without solecism, in a neighbouring woodland, lyrically described in a slim volume by a celebrated amateur golfer. Scattered among the fertilizer, it may be remembered in Glades of Remembrance—or forgotten in Glades of Forgetfulness—where on rustic garden seats visitors meditate on other matters. And that will be that.

LORD KINROSS

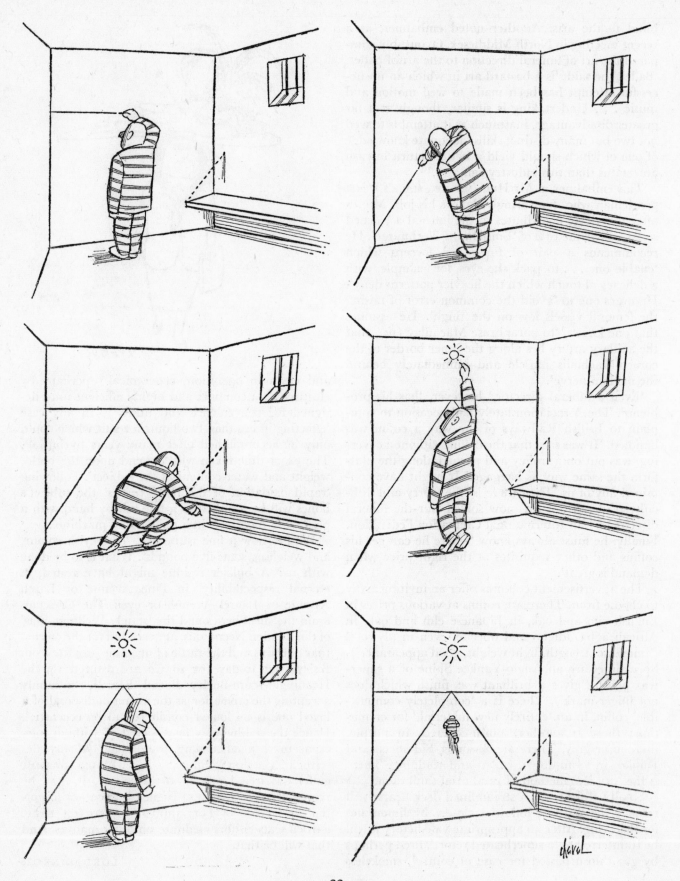

Towards a Reasoned Economy

THESE remarks are not addressed to any whose life, work or point of view removes them altogether from the grey world of reality. Politicians, captains of industry, lunatics and gipsies should pay them no heed at all. Nor will they be of the slightest value to tycoons with fat expense accounts, or to those supernaturally fortunate at Monte Carlo, or to the artistic and mobile who spend six months and a day of each year at Torremolinos. They are intended purely as aid and comfort to thinking men and women who have to live on a fixed income and—even sadder in the world of to-day—at a fixed address. Such people will have to practise a stringent economy from now to the end of their lives if the privileged classes listed above are to continue making ends meet; and this being so, it is worth taking pains to establish the best, the most imaginative, way of going about it.

A method that will occur to some is by not spending money; and there may be those who will allege that it is the most reliable. But here is a frame of mind we must try to avoid. In the system I am about to lay before you there is no place for crankiness of that sort, or any other. It is scientific, and yet allows the fancy to play; it depends on rational control, and yet involves no hardship; and it is simple. Laughably simple, you may think, when you hear the formula: Intelligent Saving, Prudent Investment.

You may remember the gasp of horror that went up some time ago when it was announced that gin was to be a few shillings dearer: the care-lined faces, the muttering, the anxious working out of sums on the backs of old envelopes. As far as I was concerned the system immediately got to work with its usual oiled precision. By not drinking gin at all I was the price of at least one bottle a week to the good already, and the extra cost therefore merely represented an additional saving! and I now was able to afford a good dry sherry instead of the African brew of leaner times.

Now please don't say that this is no good to you because you do drink gin. Only have patience, and rum or whisky will go up. One of the few things in contemporary life on which we may rely, absolutely, is a steady rise in all prices all the time. But every individual doesn't spend on every commodity or service, and the saving he effects in this way must steadily rise as well. A staggering increase in bus fares brings welcome relief to the man who runs a powerful car: if the price of petrol be doubled, it is a real little windfall for the man who drives a pony and trap. Thus, with things as they are, we simply cannot lose.

Another way of saving, equally fool-proof, is to spend every penny the minute you get it. What costs a pound to-day will certainly cost twenty-two and sixpence in twelve months' time, and who but a madman pays half a crown more for a thing than he need? And suppose you put that pound away in the Post Office, as some frantic individuals will urge you to do, who is going to give you half a crown interest at the end of the year to preserve the *status quo*? You will have to be content with sixpence: so that every pound you spend to-day is a clear two shillings in your pocket, *and* there is no need to hang about waiting for it to fall due.

Sound as all this is, however, there is something a little mechanical about it. It calls for no ingenuity but arises simply and inevitably from the conditions

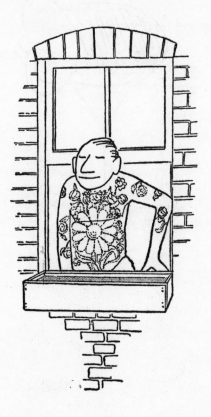

of the day. Let us now go on to consider the system in its truly creative aspect.

We will begin by budgeting for an evening's entertainment: we have invited a friend to dinner and the play, and the question is, how much to draw out of the bank. Two pounds a head should cover the meal, so make it three as oysters are still in season: that's six. Theatre tickets, seventeen and sixpence each, but call it a pound as fractions are so confusing. Thirty shillings should cover programmes and light refreshments: but will it? This is to be a gala evening and we mustn't pare cheese. A couple of pounds, then, and there ought to be a little reserve as well, in case of contingencies. The total stands at ten, and we had better make the reserve another five, as it is easier to add up the counterfoils when the amounts end in 5 or 0. Capital! Off we go to the bank. Then our friend telephones to say he is terribly sorry, he has got to go to America. We are left in the lurch—*planté*, as they say in France—with fifteen pounds on our hands, plus the thirty shillings increment we have earned by not waiting until next year.

Some people lose their heads at a moment like this and fritter the money away on grocery bills or in similar excess; but we have long had our eye on a little musical-box. The price of it is twenty pounds and we unexpectedly have sixteen-pound-ten towards it. Is seventy shillings too much to pay for so charming a thing, that will look so well with our other musical-boxes, and that we could leave to our children, if only we had them? But just as we are purring over our luck there comes a sudden appalling realization of our selfishness and indifference to others. Merely because we happen to be on a diet it never even occurred to us that our friend would probably have liked some supper after the play. We were on the point of allowing this dear friend of ours, to whom we owe so much, to have gone hungry to bed; and in our remorseful desire to make amends we see that only the best would have done for him. Now, therefore, we get the musical-box for nothing, and still have a pound or so in hand.

The beauty of the transaction is that it leaves the way open to further investment. We should have had that musical-box sooner or later in any case: as it is, we have both the box and a capital gain of twenty pounds. Unless our friend should telephone again to say he is not going to America after all—and he is not a man to chop and change—we may go confidently forward on our career of reasoned purchase with a twenty-pound discount on every single outlay: the future is smiling at us.

HONOR TRACY

24

Spatterdash

THE HORROR COMES CLOSER

IT WAS about a fortnight after the great darkness had enveloped all the southern counties of England, and the Government, despairing alike of agricultural labour and transport, had already decided to issue portions of medicated smog as a national food, when my friend Tiger Mackinnon, gazing into the spectroscope of his dynamometer, suddenly started back in his chair.

I could see the beads of perspiration standing out on his forehead above the band of the pig-snout which our biogenetic investigations had long compelled us to wear.

'By God, Spatterdash!' he exclaimed. 'I knew it! I knew it!'

'What is biting you?' I asked.

'The spacial co-ordinates!'

'Ammonia?' I cried. 'Niobium? Absquatulation? or could it be——?'

'x,' he muttered hoarsely, 'equals x^1+v^t, $y=y^1$, $z=z^1$!'

'And then?'

'$\log bn + \log bn_1 = \log bnn_1$, $\log bn - \log bn_1 = \log b\frac{u}{u_1}l_1$. $\log bn = \log b \, (nl^1)$!'

I could see that his senses were leaving him. 'You mean that this is not our smog after all?'

'Only partly. It is seeping in from outer relativity.

A meteorite has crept up under cover of our obfuscated atmosphere and is spraying it with differential calculi.'

'Dial 999!'

He did so. There was nothing but a buzzing sound. That was how The Terror began.

THE STAMP OF DOOM

It was a few days later that my daughter Iphigenia stole into the laboratory, pale as an arum lily, and touched my arm. I could see that she had been weeping.

'It is about Paul,' she said. 'He took off his pig-snout!'

'The fool, what for?'

'To kiss me,' she murmured, blushing like a peony. 'And then he changed suddenly and said that he loved me no longer. And there was a mark on his forehead.'

'What sort of mark?'

'Pi.'

'Pie?'

'The Greek letter.'

I tried to hide my emotion, but the tears trickled down under my snout.

LORD UTTERMORE ACTS

It was the same everywhere. The poison from the meteorite, which we called Bollonion, transformed the character of everyone who inhaled its miasmatic effluvium. Politics were thrown into confusion. The three principal leaders of the Labour party entered the House of Commons arm in arm, singing 'Auld Lang Syne'. The Conservative Prime Minister made a long speech defending Enosis in Sark. The worst elements of the population thrived on the vapour, the noblest sickened and died. Rabbits reappeared exhibiting remarkable ferocity, and ran about the city devouring cats and dogs. The pulpits were deserted. Forehead after forehead showed the terrible traces of π.

On the very day that Parliament decided to suspend Christmas, Lord Uttermore, the great newspaper proprietor, summoned me to his office.

'I have decided,' he said, 'to attack Bollonion at once.'

'But all the regular rocket services are cancelled, my lord.'

'I know it, Spatterdash. We will travel in my own private rocket. I have had it tipped with Silenium, and reinforced with Amygdaloid.'

I breathed a mineralogical prayer.

'Impossible,' I said at last.

'Not at all. The point has been specially sharpened with emery paper. Put on your armour at once!'

'Armour?' I ejaculated.

'I have borrowed the best suits of armour from the Tower. We shall carry two sten guns loaded with uranium, two maces and three oxygen pumps. Your daughter Iphigenia will accompany us.'

'I entreat you——'

'The woman's point of view is most necessary. Her photographs are in my papers to-night. You may like

to know that your friend Mackinnon has been arrested for rioting.'

'Tiger Mackinnon?'

'There has been a strike of astronomers and Greenwich Observatory is in ruins. The B.B.C. have had to cancel their weather report.'

I could but gasp and obey.

THE TERRIBLE JOURNEY

We went up and up. How we penetrated the toughness of that terrible murk I shall never understand. It seemed eons before we emerged like a tube train running out of a tunnel into the clear realms of space and beheld from the conning-tower of our rocket the icy tundras of Bollonion. Through an awful chasm in the meteorite's side we saw, flowing like lava, the venomous ooze designed to infect our planet. The pump was being operated by slimy shapes of indescribable foulness with writhing antennæ in the shape of algebraical formulæ. I dashed to one of the sten guns and was about to fire when I observed with the tail of my eye the menacing attitude of Lord Uttermore. He had seized one of the maces and was about to attack me. I turned like a panther and evaded him. His eyes were those of a maniac, and clear on his forehead stood the awful sign.

'I have decided to land on Bollonion,' he shouted, 'and integrate it with Earth.'

Using a woman's swift intuition Iphigenia handed me the second mace. The rocket had been slowed down and we seemed to fight for hours, but finally I thrust Lord Uttermore so violently against one of the plate glass windows that it broke. He balanced a moment, screamed and fell. At the same moment Iphigenia, shutting her eyes, discharged one of the sten guns. There was a terrific explosion and I knew no more.

THE DARKNESS ENDS

When I became conscious I was in hospital. Paul and Iphigenia were bending over me, and the young man's brow was as clear as ivory. All the smog had gone.

'Luckily,' said my daughter, 'I found the right lever for putting the rocket in reverse. But what,' she added with a touch of contrition, 'can have happened to Lord Uttermore?'

I smiled. 'He must be spinning eternally round the Universe, I suppose.'

'Poor man.'

'I don't feel so certain. He has never had a circulation like that before.'

EVOE

26

Thoughts on the Diary of a Nobody

THE POOTERS walked to Watney Lodge
  One Sunday morning hot and still
Where public footpaths used to dodge
  Round elms and oaks to Muswell Hill.

That burning buttercuppy day
  The local dogs were curled in sleep,
The writhing trunks of flowery May
  Were polished by the sides of sheep.

And only footsteps in a lane
  And birdsong broke the silence round
And chuffs of the Great Northern train
  For Alexandra Palace bound.

The Watney Lodge I seem to see
  Is gabled gothic, hard and red,
With here a monkey puzzle tree
  And there a round geranium bed.

Each mansion, each new-planted pine,
  Each short and ostentatious drive
Meant Morning Prayer and beef and wine
  And Queen Victoria alive.

Dear Charles and Carrie, I am sure,
  Despite that awkward Sunday dinner,
Your lives were good—and more secure
  Than ours at cocktail time in Pinner.

JOHN BETJEMAN

27

After 'Family Portrait'

The following correspondence between the Stewards of the Jockey Club and the Director of the British Broadcasting Corporation has been issued to the Press:

AT a meeting of the Jockey Club the play recently shown on Television, *Derby Round*, was discussed and it was decided to send you a formal protest.

The play is false in material fact and is repugnant to all lovers of racing.

1. It represents the Derby Stakes as a steeplechase when in fact it is, and always has been, run on the flat.

2. Stewards of the Jockey Club are shown taking bribes from trainers.

3. Jockeys are shown equipped with electric devices in spurs and whip. All the horses were drugged. The owners carry pistols and threaten 'bookies' into changing the odds.

4. The party in the Royal Box is shown to be intoxicated.

All this, we submit, is not truly representative of English racing. To show this play on Derby Night, after your excellent running commentary on the race, was considered an additional affront . . .

BROADCASTING HOUSE
We are in no doubt that a grave error was made in showing the play on Derby night. Its repetition on

'To think we'd be rolling in money if you hadn't frightened the horse!'

subsequent nights is a different matter and we propose to repeat it, with a preface stating that it does not pretend to reconstruct the historical happenings of this or any other particular race.

The Times: next day

SIR,—Many besides myself will have been shocked by the apologetic tone adopted by the Director of the B.B.C. towards the Jockey Club. Who are they to say that 'racing' is synonymous with 'horse racing'? For the few hundreds, many of them foreigners, who are concerned in the former activity there are countless thousands to whom 'racing' means the sport to which my Society is dedicated.

Yours, etc.,
ANTHONY JERK, *Secretary*
The Society of English Pigeon Trainers

SIR,—As one who has never been to a horse race of any kind may I say that *Derby Round* seemed to me a singularly moving play and one which has greatly increased my love of owners, trainers, jockeys, bookies and horses?

Your obedient servant,
JANE BROWN

The Times: next day

SIR,—*Derby Round* was drama. Drama is Art. Art knows no frontiers . . .

Yours sincerely,
JAM BHU
President of Anglo-Oriental Writers Interdiscussion Union

The Times: next day

SIR,—All humanists must deplore the attempt of a small section of the public to bring pressure upon a publicly-owned corporation. We in this country give our permission to the Jockey Club to conduct their own affairs in their own way provided they do not interfere with our liberties and comfort. One of our most precious liberties is to see others held up to ridicule and contempt. The precise objections are not of first importance. It seems that many agree with the Jockey Club in believing that the Derby is a flat race. The fact that this opinion is not universally held is attested by the authors of *Derby Round*. It is only by hearing all opinions that a democratic citizen can reach his own decision.

Your obedient Servants,
SAM GROSS, REG CUTTLE, NICK RUDD
The Thermobiological Institute, Cambridge

New Statesman: next weekend

London Diary

So grievously shocking was the slavish apology offered by the B.B.C. to the Jockey Club that the remedy is violence. This is still a nation of horses— and by horses I include all men and animals who are not themselves the owners of racehorses . . .

Critic

Same journal, correspondence column

It is a fact that until a few years ago the Derby Stakes was always a steeplechase. It was held at Aintree Course, Goodwood. There is ample proof of this in my late father's well known work *Joanna Southcott and the Great Pyramid*. Excavations now in progress at Harringay, which I have been privileged to see, leave no doubt of the question. The Jockey Club in recent years have sought to destroy all evidence of this truth. But when the Harringay report. . . .

EVELYN WAUGH

'*You surely don't suppose I'm going to allow mere proof to sway my opinion.*'

The Old, Old Ladies of 1956

WHEN I look at the old, old ladies
  Whose hair is completely grey,
I think with a sigh: I wonder, will I
  Be exactly like them one day?

Will *I* have to cross the Sahara?
  Or walk round the floor on my hands?
Or wander afloat in a small open boat
  Among barely pronounceable lands?

Will *I* have to stand for election
  And sit up till dawn spinning words?
Will *I* have to tramp through the fog and the damp
  To study the habits of birds?

When *I* am an old, old lady
  And my hair is completely grey,
Oh, please, can I sit by the fire and knit
  Just as I do to-day?

CELIA FREMLIN

Paranormally Speaking

NOTHING but good can come of the free and frank discussion between nations of ghostly occurrences and paranormal phenomena generally. We tend to be too insular in these matters. A Bulgarian ghost, to take a phantom at random, may well be quite different from ours. Swiss ghosts, one suspects, are often roped together, and only clank when seated in spectral rack-and-pinion coaches driven by headless Motor-men. To a Greek, an ordinary English ghost, properly sheeted, would look like Demosthenes; and in Morocco it might pass altogether without remark.

A great opportunity for widening international understanding in the phenomenal field appeared to be afforded by the recent conference of the New York Foundation of Para-Psychology, held (by courtesy of the British Society of Psychical Research) at Newnham College, Cambridge, and attended by twenty-nine delegates, mostly from universities in Europe and America. Subjects on the Agenda included 'Poltergeists: History and Methods of Investigation' and 'Phantasms of the Living and the Dead: the Traditional Method of Research'. But the opportunity has, in large measure, been wantonly cast away by the decision of the conference to exclude all pressmen and visitors and to hold their meetings in secret session. If the following account of its deliberations (sent by our representative, who got in with great difficulty disguised as a Doctor of Demonology from Leipzig and was eventually betrayed by his accent) is scanty and inaccurate, the conference has only itself to thank.

* * *

THE SPANISH DELEGATE: Well-authenticated cases of mule-bells following *bona fide* travellers in the Sierra de Guadarrama are on record in the proceedings of my Society. When they turned round there was nothing there.

A PROFESSOR OF PARA-PSYCHOLOGY AT VIENNA: Ghastly.

THE RUSSIAN DELEGATE: We know nothing of such goings-on in my country. I have many times been awoken by the rumble of tanks and on looking out of my window have counted up to two hundred, which in Russian takes much time. In the morning, although it was snowing, there were no tracks. It is proved. The matter is not for discussion.

A CAMBRIDGE DON: I say, have any of you fellows been haunted by sheep? A friend of mine whose veracity I can vouch for was returning home late from the Fitzwilliam. It was a moonless night, one of those nights when the trees stand like gaunt black sentinels along the road and a kind of still watchfulness, a sense not of Presences exactly but of the *imminence* of something restrained, held back, presses in upon the solitary walker. As he strode along his attention was arrested by a bleat or baa, coming from a point to one side and a little—and to this my friend is prepared to swear—a little *above* him, so that——

THE HERR PROFESSOR OF PHANTASMAGORIA AND KINDRED SCIENCES AT DRESDEN: The delegate has said bleat *or* baa. It is necessary to be precise in such matters.

CAMBRIDGE DON: The terms are synonymous in Cambridge. Quickening his pace, for though not an impressionable man——

THE CHAIRMAN: We are wandering from the point. The paper for discussion before the Conference is 'Impalpability and Formlessness: Is Something Enough?'

CAMBRIDGE DON: This sheep was neither felt nor seen. My point is that a disembodied bleat, or baa if the Herr Professor will allow me, is a paranormal phenomenon, and as such a proper subject for investigation.

THE DELEGATE FROM HARVARD: Permit me to attempt a brief appraisal of progress as of now. Dr Coldheim, in his very interesting and stimulating paper, advanced the proposition—a somewhat revolutionary proposition, gentlemen—that the Impalpable must have Shape. 'Let us discountenance,' he says in effect, 'all so-called phenomena that cannot be more accurately described than as Something, a Thing, It, or even "a swirling mass of darkness that seemed to dilate and condense about its yet blacker centre".' He advises us to leave such vague manifestations to the fiction-writers. Now we on the Eastern Seaboard——

SENHOR FERNANDO DE BRUNHA (*Lisbon*): We should ban Mass and Impact. Things that blunder against people in the dark bring the whole business into disrepute.

AN OXFORD DELEGATE: Oh, come! Do you disbelieve in poltergeists? I could show you bruises——

PROFESSOR OF P-Ps. AT VIENNA: What about smell? I am continually being asked to investigate icy cold draughts accompanied by a faint musty odour.

THE DUTCH REPRESENTATIVE: I should now wish to speak of mysterious blotches on walls. Myself, I am recently called in to advise some good people in Amsterdam.

A VOICE: It eventually transpired that the previous tenant had been foully done to death in that very room.

THE CHAIRMAN (*sharply*): Who said that?

CAMBRIDGE DON: The voice seemed to come from behind and a little above me. Reverting to my original point, there is a woman still alive in Ipswich who a few years ago distinctly heard the neigh of her favourite horse, which passed over in 1896. Much work remains to be done in the field of palæophonic manifestations, particularly with relation to the animal kingdom.

A SMALL NORWEGIAN: Trolls——

THE CHAIRMAN (*loudly*): I now call upon the delegate from Aberdeen to read his paper on 'Clamminess: Its Use and Abuse as an Aid to the Identification of Phantasmata.'

A VOICE: Could you repeat the last word, please?

THE CHAIRMAN: Quick! There he is! Throw that ghastly manifestation out.

H. F. ELLIS

33

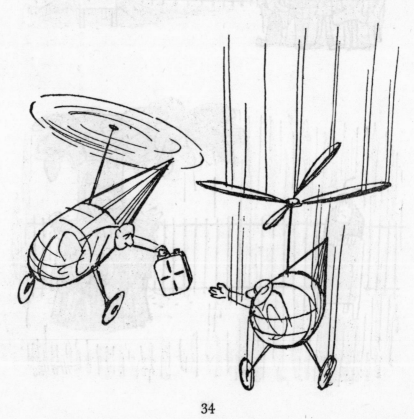

Writer's Mail

A WRITER's mail is very interesting, but gradually over the years the letters fall into categories. The most common is the fan letter, written simply because the writer, after reading something of mine, has felt the urge to communicate. These letters usually begin, 'I have never written a fan letter before'. I wonder why that is always said. It is a little like the man who asks for an autograph never for himself but for his little daughter.

Then there is the letter which starts out with praise and then gets to work on my morals and choice of subject—'There is so much that is beautiful and pure in the world,' it says, 'why do you have to stir up ugliness and filth?'

A third kind of letter is the honest out-and-out denunciation. A great many of these utilize four-letter words and say real bad things. One man was so mad at me that he ended his letter: 'Beware. You will never get out of this world alive.'

Then come the requests for autographs and pictures—some of them naïve and some of them quite professional. These latter usually list the signatures they already have, including Thomas Mann—nearly always—and George Bernard Shaw. The implication is that I will be in good company if I send it and a schmuck if I don't. One man sent me fifty slips of paper to sign. He was honest. He said he was going to trade them with other collectors.

Of course there are a great many thoughtful and intelligent letters—sometimes having to do with some phase of my work which has interested the writer or to which he can contribute some information. Many of these are good and warming to receive.

The requests for money are fairly constant, though reaching their peak a few months after each book is published. Some of these seem genuine, but many others are straight hustles and not very clever. One time I received a collect wire from a man I had never heard of demanding that I send four hundred dollars by return wire for an operation. I very naturally ignored it. The next day, another wire came saying two hundred and fifty dollars would be sufficient if sent immediately. Again I was silent with flying money. In a few days I had a letter from this claimant. He said he had always admired me, but now he found I had clay feet.

There are always the bughousers—fortunately, not many, but nearly always repeaters. I answered a letter from a woman who said she was one hundred and one years old, and got a completely illegible postcard from her every day for a year. I made out of the scrawl that pretty soon she got me confused with her son who had died fifty years before. Then I had one pen pal who claimed she was married to me. And another who wrote often for a while and said that Joan Crawford was her mother and Bing Crosby her father and they wouldn't give her any money so she appealed to me, her uncle, to ask them to send her fifty thousand dollars. I got quite a few letters from that one and she enclosed pictures of herself. She was pretty, if the pictures were of her.

There are the letters asking for further information on a subject on which you have written, and others pointing out errors. In *East of Eden* I made an error in the spelling of Tinshol. I spelled it Tinshel. I have had over a hundred letters pointing out my mistake and many of them from profound scholars of Hebrew.

One of the commonest experiences to a writer is to be invited to act as collaborator. My mail is studded with such suggestions. The letters usually start—'I have had a very interesting life if someone would just sit down and write it up'. The writer does not say why his story is interesting, being convinced and sometimes saying openly that unless contractually bound I might steal his material. The letters nearly always end with this business proposition: 'You write it up and get it published and we'll split fifty-fifty.'

Some of the letters hint of dark political secrets, some of crime and injustice in high places, some of sin-strewn careers. Invariably, the correspondent suggests a meeting face to face when I will be given the fascinating material. There seems to be no suspicion that I might just as well steal it then as earlier. The letter always starts with the high moral implications to be served by such a work, but the end never fails to mention the fifty-fifty split of the loot.

I have had such letters from all kinds of people—convicts, old ladies who remember seeing Lincoln, ministers, doctors, dreamers, realists. I remember one letter, however, I liked very much and which tempted me. It went: 'Dear Bud, I got a million stories. I run a saloon out in —— and the God-damndest things happen here. We could make a fortune just writing them down. You come out here and see. I'll stake you to grub and liquor. If you have a wife she can tend bar while we write.' It was hard to refuse that one.

Then there was a whole series of letters from a man-and-wife flagpole-sitting team. Their courtship had been on adjoining flagpoles in a contest. Then they got together and were married on a flagpole, and at the time of the letters they were planning to have a baby one hundred and twenty feet in the air. They needed an historian, and hinted that if I could pull it off the money would roll in.

I thought that would be hard to top, but recently I received a letter so meaty that I put it down in its entirety. The letterhead said, 'World Champion Lady Wrestler,' and it went as follows:

'DEAR MR STEINBECK,—After reading some of your books, I believe you are the proper person for me to contact.

I want to write a story based on my life and the twenty years I have spent in my profession. Not a story to particularly put myself over but one that pulls no punches on the inside of girl wrestling.

I have had many writers approach me for a story but I always had to protect my profession and besides no one can write what you have lived for twenty years but yourself.

My story would carry tremendous impact and if properly written will make a terrific picture.

At first I just wanted to write it myself and then have it rewritten properly as I would not have the ability on the finer points of writing.

But I am in very serious financial trouble's and must have $5,000.00 to pay debt's immediately and money to exist on while writing. I have been offered up to $1,000.00 for short scandle stories and have turned it down as that would take the edge off my book. If you are able to invest £5,000.00 which I know is small money to what could be made from the book, the first $5,000.00 made could go to you and after that we could split 50–50 on everything.

If you want you can have full credit for the book under your name, as I am only trying to keep myself out of trouble. Of course my career will be finished after this book is published, I mean my wrestling career, that is why I must be sure to get something out of it, also I must have the money soon as my situation is critical.

Of course I would talk it over with you first so you could see I really have something to write about, something that would probably shock you.

Please let me hear from you by return mail, because if you are not interested I must try to find someone who is and who has the ability to do it right. Everyone can not write this type of story and I am sure you will do it justice.

Hoping to hear from you by return mail.'

You know, I like the direct approach of this broad. She lays it on the line, and in my mind I have already cast the picture. I know some lady wrestlers in Hollywood—amateurs. I am pleased that she thinks I have the ability to do her story justice, but I am afraid that again I must decline.

JOHN STEINBECK

The Guide Punchelin

WELCOME TO BRITAIN

VISITORS from abroad will find a warm welcome in Britain, with eager hands outstretched on all sides. Show your friendly response by putting money in these. Remember that you can't get a drink in the afternoons, that every town has its free car park if you have enough petrol to get you there, and that after certain hours a *delicatessen* cannot sell sandwiches, only separate bread and meat to make your own. Also note the following:

BRITISH ROADS

These are of three kinds, main, by and up. The compilers of the Atlas (pp. 860-895) cannot be responsible for changes made after going to press, by which time all roads may be up. Small black figures in a circle denote average traffic-jam times in minutes. Coach roads are marked (*c*), denoting their continuous use by forty-seater coaches travelling to and from the sea in convoys of twenty at 55 m.p.h.

PLACES OF INTEREST

For the first time the Guide includes mention of galas, etc., opened by well-known television personalities. Tourists confining their sight-seeing to Britain's many fine 'new towns' should get a route from another source. Clearly the Guide cannot include details of communities springing up overnight.

HOTELS

Though the Guide attempts to convey in advance the quality of the British Hotel this remains at the last a matter of individual taste. Where specialities of cuisine are mentioned the reader must decide for himself whether an enticement or a warning is intended.

Any comments on hotels should be sent to the British Travel and Holidays Association, remembering that it is illegal in Britain to send obscene matter through the mails.

SYMBOLS USED IN THE GUIDE PUNCHELIN

General

Bomb damage

Litter black spot

U.S.A.A.F. personnel

Fish shop

Drainage scheme

Slot machine arcade

Stately home

Teddy boys

Speed Trap

Dimbleby slept here

N.H.S. doctor

N.H.S. surgeon

N.H.S. psychiatrist

T.V. dealer

Church used by Royalty

Factory

Municipal statue

Polite shopkeeper

Hotels

De luxe

Typical

Homely

Dancing below room

Good view

Nice view

View

Sidings nearby

Town clock strikes

Town clock strikes and chimes

Water-pipe noise

Claims oldest waiter

Resident bore

Golf centre

Oak beams

Boots cleaned

Dry beds

Viewing room

Tooth glasses

Warm toast

Cuisine

Eatable

Homely

Deadly

Tea-bags

Warm beer

'OK' Claret (1955)

'Little Wonder' cigars

Eau de potage

Porridge aux lumpes

Separate pastry

Dainty teas

Garages

Smithy type

Punctures only

Usually closed

Unmanned

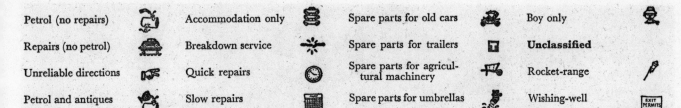

Petrol (no repairs)   Accommodation only   Spare parts for old cars   Boy only

Repairs (no petrol)   Breakdown service   Spare parts for trailers   **Unclassified**

Unreliable directions   Quick repairs   Spare parts for agricul-   Rocket-range
                                                       tural machinery

Petrol and antiques   Slow repairs   Spare parts for umbrellas   Wishing-well   EXIT PERMITS

GT. FROWSTON-BY-BINGLINGSLEY

Typical old English village with village hall (*c.* 1898). To the east, interesting old lumps in Marley's Meadow, thought to be tombs of Saxon Kings or possibly disused air-raid shelters. Home of Mr F. Bether at 23 High Street, successful 'What's My Line?' challenger; plaque affixed. Sir Thomas More's daughter once had a drink at 'The Lamb'. Interesting old thatched houses, 'The Gatchens' (if still standing). Modern concrete lamp-standards. Twenty-two public houses, two hotels with interesting old waitresses.

Hotels

King's Head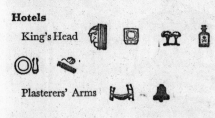

Plasterers' Arms

Garages

There are no garages, but horses may be hired by the hour; Capt. Sapper, 'Cob House.' Tel.: 2.

SKEGPOOL-ON-SEA

Typical watering-place. 28 cinemas, eight variety theatres, 12 dance-halls, two piers, one repertory theatre (at time of going to press), four ice-rinks, three greyhound stadiums, eight bathing-pools. For music-lovers, the Beethoven Trio, 4 p.m.-4.30 p.m. in West Pier Concertorium, alternate days. At nearby Eastcliffe, the Floral Gardens and Castle Ruins (artificial, *c.* 1928). 'Have a Go' twice broadcast from Skegpool Plastics Centre, Fish Street. Municipal records give more than 200 hotels, of which the following are representative.

Hotels

Grand Savoy-Carlton

Central Conference

The Grosvenor

Garages

Most of these are ▤ as Skegpool's visitors tend to buy afresh rather than have old cars repaired. Note may however be taken of *All-Nite Garage* ✳ and *Conquest Motors.*

CROWNCHESTER

Typical industrial town. Sleeps during Wakes Week. Many cultural centres include the Sir Herbert Chelp Museum, the Percy Trumley Art Gallery and the W. H. Vokins Botanical Gardens. Statue in Trumley Avenue is unique in showing a late Alderman in robes on horseback, with drawn sword (Sir H. Chelp). Other entertainments: ice- and roller-rinks 'freshwater' fishing (Crownchester Canal) dancing (Ritz Ballroom, Engine Street). Also see Keir Hardie House for permanent exhibition of Strike Notices.

Hotels

Chelp Arms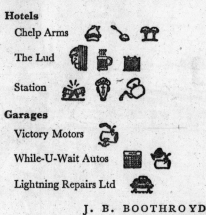

The Lud

Station

Garages

Victory Motors

While-U-Wait Autos

Lightning Repairs Ltd

J. B. BOOTHROYD

Have You Ever Ridden in a Tram?

THERE are still places in the quiet backwaters of Britain where communication between one district and another is made by the old-fashioned electric tram.

People who do not know them cannot imagine the curious old-world grace with which these dignified vehicles glide along the gleaming tracks that line the cobbled streets in many an outlying metropolis in Britain's ever-surprising isle.

They seem at once exotic and homely as they

growl and clang their way past the long terraces of humble homesteads, from pub to railway station, from cricket field to chapel. *Ting!*—and Mrs Ormondroyd has the fourpenny ticket that will take her to the gasworks. *Ting!*—and Mr Huyton is on his way to the post office to collect his pension.

They're friendly vehicles, trams, as friendly as the folk who man them and the folk who ride them. It is worth making a detour to get to know them.

Drop in and see your travel agent *now*. He will be glad to give you any further advice you require.

For further information and free literature, write the British Travel Association.

B. A. YOUNG

Mother of Seven

I CANNOT tell you how the thing occurred
　Or when, in point of fact, it all began.
I only heard what everybody heard:
　MOTHER OF SEVEN ALARMED BY LIMPING MAN.

I cannot say what else the facts disclosed,
　Whether his face alarmed her or his gait,
And what connection is to be supposed
　Between her married and her mental state.

None, I suspect. Not all the writer's art
　Could weave much fabric from this fertile wife.
Nothing she had could hold the public heart
　But this florescence in her private life.

And this not long. Sad though it often is,
　Romance and ripeness cannot co-exist;
Too frequent and too fruitful pregnancies
　Distract spectator and protagonist.

Reiteration blunts the greatest good,
　And men prize mostly what they most intend.
No one who gloried in her motherhood
　Could glory in it seven times on end.

Contrast there was, a hint of light and shade,
　Some touch of freshness in the story told:
She now made news who hitherto had made
　Seven children only in the self-same mould.

But that was all. The limping man was seen
　At Slough and Streatham Hill, but never spoke.
Her motherhood remained what it had been,
　Her cross, her secret pride, the local joke.

She sighed, and put her cuttings-book away
　Among her souvenirs, and turned, half-vexed
And half-refreshed, as from a holiday,
　To what, on form, she knew must happen next.

P. M. HUBBARD

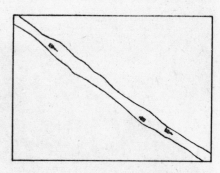

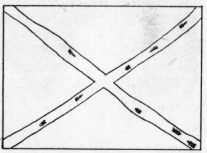

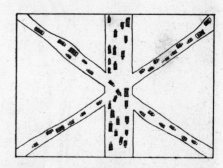

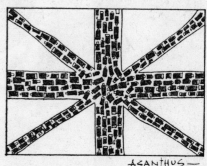

A history of English road development

America Day by Day

Down where I live, on the south shore of Long Island, things have been pretty quiet of late, and will continue so till this year's hurricanes come along and blow us cross-eyed, but elsewhere in America there has been quite a bit of stir and excitement. I am not thinking so much of the activities of H. B. Nielson, who—no doubt for the sake of the wife and kiddies—recently rolled a marble six miles in ninety minutes, though this has received wide publicity, as of the re-opening of the Harrison, New Jersey, drawbridge over the Passaic river.

You know how these drawbridges work. A boat comes along and toots. You press a button, the bridge goes up, the boat goes through, you press another button and the bridge comes down again. And about as pleasant a way of passing the long summer days as one could imagine. But in 1946, having opened to allow a tanker to pass through, this Harrison bridge stayed open and remained that way for ten years. Then the Essex and Hudson Board of Freeholders, who never stand that sort of thing indefinitely, clubbed together and raised $342,239 to have it put back into working order, and the big day for the reopening ceremony was fixed. The Mayor was there. There was a silver band. Speeches were made, the Star-spangled Banner sung, and schoolchildren paraded in droves, many of them with clean faces. Somebody handed the Mayor the scissors to cut the ribbon, and at that moment, just as he was saying, 'I hereby declare that everything from now on is going to be just as mother made it,' a tanker tooted. Up went the bridge, and stayed up. If they ever get it down again, I'll let you know.

Turning to America's crime wave, it seems to be receding. In New York the Police Commissioner's report shows a reduction of 16·5 per cent in major crimes. Either murderers and burglars are loafing on their job, or the cops are copping with extra vigour. At any rate, it is at last possible to go for an evening stroll without having some teen-ager come along and hold you up and stick lighted matches between your toes, a practice which in the past has caused numerous complaints. But there is always something. *Surgit*, as the old Roman said, *aliquid amari*. The criminal classes, though easing up a little

in their operations, have become distressingly slipshod in their speech. The other day there were two hold-ups, one at the Pennsylvania station, the other in a bar. Both bandits said, 'This is a stick-up!' and then one of them went on, 'Everybody keep their seats.' The other bandit said, 'Everybody put their hands up.' Watch it, boys, watch it. Not 'their'. 'Everybody keep *his* seat. Everybody put *his* hands up.' If you have to rob people, well and good, no doubt you need the money. But do be grammatical about it. Get your *Fowler* and make of it a constant companion.

The criminals will argue, I suppose, that it is better, even if it strikes a jarring note on a sensitive ear, to make your meaning clear than just to take the English language and tie it into lover's knots as the Madison Avenue advertising men do. There is some justice in this. I append a letter from an employee in an advertising firm to the head of the organization. There appears to have been some hitch in the smooth running of the firm's business, and the letter runs as follows:

'Dear Boss,

Well, I bet you were about to give me the crossed wrists on this little sally, but the boys from Stratford had a rhubarb with the fact-finders and we all got hung up for awhile waiting for the matador to clear the field so the picadors could punch the clock. Even then, Chief, for my coin of the realm the whitewash cabinet was strictly Mother Hubbard, and as you can see from these warm-ups, the main event is longshot to get even a whisper from the ringsiders. From this end of the eyeglass, Top, that Michelangelo is not only O.T.L. but G.F.T.D., and I'm sure you'll want to give the whole thing the right lapel.'

Hold-up men would never stoop to that sort of thing. They have their pride.

Passing on to Sedalia, Missouri, where there is always something doing, we note that Station

KDRO-TV, staging a money-raising drive for the polio fund, got from one viewer the firm offer that he would pay $5 to see Patrolman Leroy Kidwell hit in the face with a custard pie. (The report does not say why, but, reading between the lines, one receives the impression that this man had got something against the zealous officer.)

With Police Chief Edgar Neighbors to think was to act. He routed Patrolman Kidwell out of bed and put it up to him.

'Not for $5,' said Mr. Kidwell firmly. 'But I'll do it for $50.'

Scarcely had his words been relayed to the public when calls started pouring in, and when the pledges reached $65, the patrolman expressed himself satisfied. He appeared on the screen, got the custard pie squarely between the eyes, wiped it off and went back to bed.

The only other incident that has stirred America lately occurred in a bar on Third Avenue (or Toid Avnoo, as it is more usually called). A man strode in and, announcing that this was his birthday, shouted, 'Drinks for everybody in the house—you, too, bartender,' and it was only after the local stags at eve had drunk their fill that the bartender suggested diffidently that to keep his records straight he would be glad if the gentleman would pay the bill.

'Bill?' said the founder of the feast. 'Pay the *bill*? Why'—here he laughed a light laugh—'I haven't any money.' Upon which, as the custom is on Toid Avnoo, the bartender took him by the scruff of the neck and the seat of the trousers and hove him into the gutter. A few moments later, having brushed himself off, the man returned, pounded the counter, repeated that it was his birthday and invited all those present to have a drink.

'Except you, bartender,' he said with a rather nasty look.

P. G. WODEHOUSE

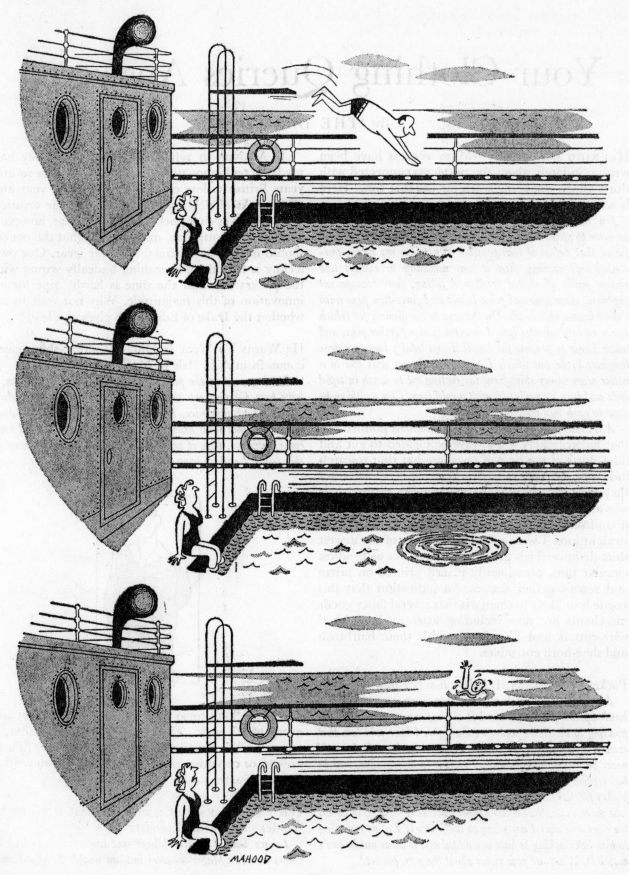

Your Clothing Queries Answered

By 'THE DANDY'

HERRING Bone Shirts?—Many readers have been writing in lately about the problems connected with shirts which are being worn for the first time. Here is a typical letter from K.L.F. (Eaton Terrace):

On returning home from the office recently with only minutes to spare in which to dress for an important dinner I found that before it was possible to get into my newly-purchased soft evening shirt it was necessary to extract two square yards of slotted cardboard filling, four transparent supports, three gummed price labels and forty-two pins with buried immovable heads. On the way to the dinner, for which I was twenty minutes late, I detected twelve further pins, and when I rose to propose the Loyal Toast totally inappropriate laughter broke out which I afterwards learnt was due to a notice sewn to my shirt-front instructing me to wash in tepid suds and iron immediately with a cold iron. Can anything be done to curb this menace?

A. A shirt manufacturer I approached pointed out that haberdashers will always be pleased to gut and fillet shirts at the time of purchase but that research indicates that the majority of customers, whatever they may say, do in fact secretly relish pitting their wits against the new shirt unit and would feel cheated if confronted with an article it was possible to get straight into. I was in fact shown some of the newest shirt designs which include such features as headless circular pins, prominently placed printed-on prices and sewn-together sleeves. An indication that this vogue is unlikely to change is that several fancy goods merchants are now including attractively finished wire-cutters and blow-lamps with their hairbrush and shoe-horn ensembles.

Pocket Problem—N.H. (Weston-super-mare) writes:

My tailor is dead keen for me to wear a small flapped bottle-opener pocket on the left side of my new suit corresponding to the ticket pocket on the right. I have told him that even if I required a bottle opener with my city suit I would never be likely to remember to keep it in this pocket, and he has replied that the fact that I have never yet used my ticket pocket for tickets has not prevented me from having one on my last three suits, that bottle-opener pockets are going to be all the rage and that I am going to look silly if I come crawling to him later asking to have one added and it turns out he can't match it. What are your views about the B.O. pocket?

A. Anxious to refute the charge that they had made no real innovations in male fashions for several years British tailors clubbed together last year and after weeks of deliberation announced the creation of the bottle-opener pocket. The public has, however, been slow to cotton on, many feeling that the pocket should have been confined to picnic wear. Our own feeling is that there is nothing basically wrong with the pocket but that the time is hardly ripe for an innovation of this magnitude. Why not wait to see whether the Duke of Edinburgh gives us a lead?

He Wants To Wear It Out!—Another shirt teaser comes from A.E. (Isle of Mull) who writes:

Having read in the paper that it was now the fashion, I have been wearing my shirt outside my trousers. Our Mum thinks I look very nice, but people I meet in the street keep sniggering and some draw me aside and whisper that I have come untucked. Can it be that I am not the type to carry off this style? I enclose snap. Please be frank.

A. The 'long torso look' admittedly does not suit every man's style. The important thing is that, if worn at all, it must be worn with confidence. (There are one or two other points about which I am writing to you privately, A.E.)

Pen Pals—A point of general interest is raised by 'Under-privileged' (Epsom):

I have bought a new blazer and am anxious to look as smart as other blazer-wearers but am unable to afford more than one good quality fountain pen and pencil to clip on to my breast pocket. Some of the lads who earn better money than I do are able to afford as many as five or six and naturally the girls prefer their company. What can I do?

A. You are in luck. A firm whose name I am supplying to you privately has realized this difficulty and has produced some very realistic inexpensive dummy pens and pencils with high-class silver-substitute heads and clips. Be warned, though : it is essential to carry at least one genuine pen and pencil among the fakes and to memorize their positions carefully!

Court Dress—G.C. (address withheld) writes:

Although a bishop I enjoy an occasional game of squash rackets. Obviously I do not wish to walk to the court, which is ten minutes distant from the Palace, in my bishop's rig-out, but equally obviously it would cause some raised eyebrows were I to make the journey dressed for squash. Can you suggest an appropriate compromise? Guidance on this problem would, I am sure, be greatly valued in countless Cathedral Closes.

A. Much attention has lately been given to this matter of providing suitable playwear for bishops and church higher-ups which combines dignity with adequate freedom and ventilation facilities, and I am happy to say that several ensembles specially designed by Tiny Tedling will soon be available in the larger department stores.

Main features of the Tedling playsuit shown here are : (*a*) white-flecked black straw boater with purple

silk band embellished with embroidered mitre, (*b*) flannel games shirt with braided modesty front counteracting plunge, (*c*) clerical grey worsted blazer

picked out with rich purple piping forming appropriate decorative motifs at key points and bordering copious collecting-bag-type pockets, (*d*) extra-roomy cream gaberdine shorts lapping naturally over (*e*) black or purple fluted stockings with lightly decorated capitals. Standard episcopal plimsolls (*f*) complete this most effective ensemble, although as shown at right a more de luxe edition of the blazer sports a stitched ecclesiastical design on the back as a timely warning to those coming up behind.

DANIEL PETTIWARD

PRODUCED, WRITTEN, DIRECTED, EDITED, ADAPTED AND NARRATED by ORSON WELLES

Académie Française

THE ACADÉMIE is on the Quai de la Seine. Everybody knows that it has always been there, that old gentlemen are sleeping in embroidered green pyjamas and feather-bonnets inside it. Down at the river, few steps lower, another association called the Clochards are working on the Argot Dictionary exerting a strong pressure on the Académiciens. The Académiciens are working since 1635 on the French Dictionary, and have now reached the letter 'B', no one is sure whether it is 'Ba' or 'Be'. Folklore says however that their main activity are 'Cocottes'. Cocottes are not entertained but built. Cocottes are the symbols of childhood. They are symbols of second childhood as well. Cocottes are paper birds massproduced by deadly-bored civil servants on their desks. Folklore says too: Académiciens are playing *saute-mouton*, catching butterflies. The Forty Immortels, The Old lady of the Quai Conty and other names glorify the place. Humorous drawings, musichall singers tell us how birds are nesting and flowers growing in the immortal beards.

However, reality as usual is stronger than fiction. The 'Immortels' don't die, they shrink. Between 1635 and 1900 there were 500 Académiciens; most of them are still there, but you can't see them; they shrank and shrank and are lodging now in inkpots, keyholes and paperbaskets. If they don't shrink, we replace. The curious thing is to watch the shrinking process. General Weygand, for instance, has not yet entered the inkpot. He was present at the 1870 war, important at the 1914-18, there still in 1940 and sitting on several Telephone Annuals, I presume, to

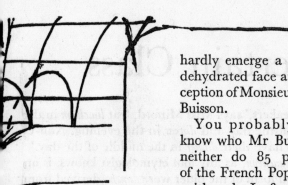

hardly emerge a pathetic dehydrated face at the reception of Monsieur Albert Buisson.

You probably don't know who Mr Buisson is, neither do 85 per cent of the French Population, neither do I after having assisted to his reception and listened for three hours: Praise speeches, and Thanksgiving speeches. All I know that he is not: Blaise Pascal, the Cathedral of Issoire, the Massif Central, nor Vercingetorix. Phrases like: 'Vermeil-enamel domes are trembling in the mist' or 'The eternal city, Roma, twice queen of the nations', are floating in the air. I understand that after having

Monsieur Albert Buisson praising his predecessor Emile Mâle

been: a Chemist, a Lawyer, a Consul, a Financier, a Writer, a Specialist of everything, he is now a Chancelier of the Académie.

Jean Cocteau is sitting and listening, his eyes shut, smiling from time to time. His own reception was in a way a 'Scandale'. If people like Cocteau enter the Académie, if the Académie is calling on people instead of people calling, and taking a lot of trouble to get in, what will happen? Receptions like the one

of Mr Buisson reassure us. In spite of this everybody considers the Académie and the Institut terribly important and prestigeful. Quite a lot of Académiciens and members of the Institut did or were doing important things, were or still are important writers. But still painters do not understand why Jean-Gabriel Domergue was made a member of the Insti-

Popular art representation of Académiciens (Canard Enchaine – tradition)

tut. His production mainly consists in paintings of young ladies with long necks and little breasts. Maybe he was considered as a pioneer in pin-up design. Pin-up designers are certainly indebted to him.

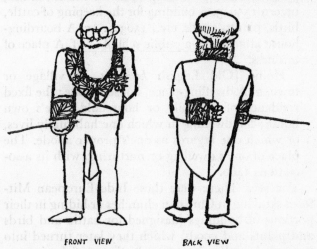

FRONT VIEW   BACK VIEW

The Jean Cocteau election only confirmed the tendency of refreshing the place. A great number of members are very much alive and go even so far as to produce films or write in Newspapers, and I do think that it is no more fashionable for celebrities to refuse to become 'de l'Académie Française'.

ANDRÉ FRANÇOIS

A Woman of a Certain Class

I HAVE only kept silent so long because the English gentleman in me shies, like one of my own hunters, at the idea of betraying a woman. But when Miss Nancy Mitford explicitly states that by a person's vocabulary you may recognize his or her class, and implicitly suggests that by her own vocabulary—e.g. the use of 'writing-paper' for 'notepaper'—we may recognize her as upper-class (U) rather than lower-middle-class (non-U), my *noblesse* refuses to *oblige*.

If language is (as I devoutly believe) an historical indicator of social status, then Miss Mitford's status as revealed by her language is open to the ghastliest misgiving. Since my own reputation as an etymologist has always been modestly confined to a limited academic circle, I prefer to emphasize this misgiving by quotation from the more widely-accepted, historically incontrovertible Oxford English Dictionary.

Miss Mitford says that 'They have a very lovely *home*' is non-U for 'They've a very nice *house*' (U).

House [con. with verbal root *hud-* of *hýdan*—to HIDE, from Indo-European stem *keudh-*] 1. A building for human habitation. b. The portion of a building occupied by one tenant or family. 2. A place of worship; a temple; a church. b. An inn, tavern 1550. 3. A building for the keeping of cattle, birds, plants, goods, etc., 1503 . . . c. A boarding-house attached to a public school . . . f. A place of business.

Home [Old English *hám*]. 1. A village or town. 2. A dwelling-place, house, abode; the fixed residence of a family or household; one's own house; the dwelling in which one habitually lives, or which one regards as one's proper abode. The place of one's dwelling or nurturing, with its associations 1460.

You see? There were these Indo-European Mitfords skulking in Christian churches or hiding in their portions of buildings (designed for cattle and birds and plants and goods) which they later turned into taverns, boarding-houses and places of business—while we Old English Dehns were dwelling and being nurtured (from about 1460 onwards) in whole villages, towns, fixed residences and proper abodes with associations. We may even, without knowing it, have harboured an Abou Ben Mitford in one of our granaries. After what fashion, you may ask, can he have lived there? Listen.

'U-speakers,' says Miss Mitford, 'eat *luncheon* in the middle of the day and *dinner* in the evening. Non-U speakers have their *dinner* in the middle of the day.'

Now *luncheon*, as any fool etymologist knows, is an expanded form of the older word *lunch* (derived from LUMP on the analogy of hump, hunch, bump, bunch.) It means: 'A piece, a thick piece.'

Luncheon. 1=LUNCH. 2. A repast taken between two meal-times, *esp.* in the morning. Still so applied by those who dine at midday. With others, *luncheon* denotes a less ceremonious meal than dinner.

Dinner [Middle English *diner*]. The chief meal of the day, eaten originally, and still by many, about midday; but now, by the fashionable classes, in the evening.

Under *Dinner*, note the pejorative antithesis between 'originally' (i.e. traditionally) and 'now' (fashionably, ephemerally). We Dehns have always kept up our mediæval family-practice of 'dining at midday', while the Mitfords (slightly referred to in the O.E.D. as 'others') less ceremoniously gnaw and chumble their thick pieces between two civilized meal-times. What do they actually eat? '*Greens*,' says Miss Mitford, 'is non-U for U *vegetables*.'

Greens. Green vegetables such as are boiled for the table 1725.

Vegetable. 1. A living organism belonging to the lower of the two series of organic beings; a growth devoid of animal life. 2. An edible herb or root used for human consumption and commonly eaten, either cooked or raw, with meat or other articles of food 1767.

Mark that 'commonly'. Half a century after my family had first eaten decently cooked greens, these upstart Mitfords arrived by caravan from God knows where behind the Karakorams and began commonly chewing roots, raw growths devoid of life, and low, living organisms. It makes one sick.

What else do they eat between meals? '*Sweet*,' says Miss Mitford, 'is non-U for U *pudding*.'

Sweet [Middle English]. 1. That which is sweet to the taste; something having a sweet taste. b. A sweet food or drink.

Pudding [Middle English *poding*, deriv. unkn.] I. 1. The stomach or one of the entrails of a pig, sheep or other animal, stuffed with minced meat, suet, seasoning, etc., boiled and kept till needed; a kind of sausage. 2. Bowels, entrails, guts. II. 1. A preparation of food of a soft or moderately firm consistency, in which the ingredients, animal or vegetable, are either mingled in a farinaceous basis, or are enclosed in a farinaceous crust, and cooked by boiling or steaming. Preparations of batter, milk and eggs, rice, sago, suitably seasoned, and cooked by baking, are now also called puddings.

It will not, I assure you, be pleasant—as I traditionally eat my sweet food and drink my sweet drink —to think of these hirsute, half-naked, Transcaucasian Mitfords spooning up great helpings of batter, rice and suitably seasoned sago or (at worst) of guts, entrails and even bowels cooked by steaming. And where, I should like to know, did they find the pigs whose stomachs they stuffed and kept (under their straw pallets?) till needed? In one of our family sties, no doubt. Tartar nomads who live furtively in portions of buildings designed for cattle are not immune from such temptations.

What do they do when they have finished their savage meal? 'Serviette,' says Miss Mitford, 'is exaggeratedly non-U usage for *napkin*.'

Now the O.E.D. is quite right in saying of *serviette*: 'latterly considered vulgar'. Naturally it was so considered—by the sort of Mongolian immigrants who reached England latterly enough to be ignorant that we born-and-bred, dyed-in-the-wool Englishmen were using the word as early (says the O.E.D.) as 1489. It means, and meant then, 'a table-napkin'. And how disturbing to find that the word *napkin*, if not preceded by the cumbersome prefix *table*-, can mean 'an infant's diaper'. It must be small comfort for Miss Mitford to know that her ancestors were at least civilized enough to *provide* their infants with diapers when she has to weigh such knowledge against the unspeakably nauseous use of these same diapers to . . . to . . . but, no. One's gorge heaves. Quick! My serviette!

Did they wash? Not, it appears, until 1656. '*Toilet*,' says Miss Mitford, is 'non-U for *lavatory*.'

Toilet. A dressing-room; in U.S. *esp.*, a dressing-room furnished with bathing facilities.

Lavatory. An apartment with apparatus for washing the hands and face; now often combined with water-closets, etc. 1656. A laundry 1661. A place for washing gold 1727.
It was in 1495, some months after Columbus's return from America, that my family installed the first New World 'toilet' at Dehn Towers. Even then it was far in advance of the primitive 'apparatus' occasionally to be found in those portions of buildings inhabited by the vagabond Mitfords. We have called it the Toilet for four and a half centuries. After 1727 we had a Lavatory too of course, but only for washing gold.

A very painful composite-picture now emerges of the Mitford sect—which I hope will finally put paid to their fantastic social pretensions. I see them, these huge, swart, hispid gipsies, after their mid-morning meal of lumps—their stomachs distended with suet and entrails, their mouths streaming with raw roots and lower organisms whose tell-tale traces they have been unable to wipe away with a hastily snatched-up baby's diaper. They rush to the washing-apparatus combined with water-closet in that portion of the cow-byre which tribal custom forbids them to call 'home'. And what do they find? Nothing but writing-paper. It's amazing that the line isn't extinct. But then barbarians are notoriously hardy.

PAUL DEHN

'*I honestly wouldn't spend another winter in England, if I were you.*'

'I understand they're sacred.'

Fiddy

Greasy Joan

WHERE is the pot that greasy Joan was keeling
    When the owl hooted? I should say it must
  Have stemmed with grease the ravages of rust
And now be hanging from some tea-shop ceiling
In or near Stratford, artlessly appealing
    To Tourists drinking tea. But Joan is dust,
And dust the man who watched her keeling, feeling
  Three parts affection and one part disgust.

The symbolized subsists, the symbol merges
    In changing facts. Joan has become a treasure,
    Diverse detergents leaving her exempt
From keeling. But amused affection purges
    Guilt; and the clinging residue of pleasure
    Cannot be keeled except with our contempt.
              P. M. HUBBARD

Through a Glass Darkly

FROM time to time it is good to look on the darker side of life. In the nineteenth century great novelists like Dickens obliged us to do so, describing with infinite pathos such humble tragedies as the hunger of Oliver Twist, the loneliness of David Copperfield and the death of Little Nell. In this age, when the way the other half lives is all too easily forgotten, the blind eye is being reopened to it, in salutary style, by the screen—or rather the two almost identical screens—of Television. Sunk in the humdrum Wonderland of our uneventful, happy-go-lucky lives, we are now faced each day with a pictorial reminder of how life is endured Through the Looking Glass.

The other world which here confronts us is a uniform, small, congested world, where men and women sit eternally, hardly moving, close together, on contemporary chairs, at desks or small tea-tables, before draped, contemporary art textiles, or strips of Regency wallpaper, or shelves of unread, dust-jacketed books, discussing or enacting, with harassed expressions, the trials of contemporary life.

It is a world of worry. Used as we are to the brave, buoyant voices of the sound radio announcers, it is a shock to us now to see their faces: the haunted eyes of the lady announcer as she reveals the weather forecast, the startled look of the gentleman announcer as he discloses that the fossilized remains of a dinosaur have been found in South Basutoland, the brave, buoyant smiles on the faces of all, which nevertheless fail to conceal a sense of deep unease.

Life, we must face it, is one long worry. The newly-wed Nortons, of Sixpenny Corner, in the rural suburb of Springwood, worry away our mornings with their hire purchase arrears, their furniture so unpresentable to visitors, Sally going and getting a cold on the eve of her birthday party, the imminent failure of Bill's garage because of his business inexperience. Grete, whom nobody wants, coming out of hospital and wanting a sit down somewhere, Stan losing his job again, Aunt Mabel in tears at winning a newspaper competition, then going up to London to spend the money, leaving Uncle Fred to mind the shop and worry away all on his own.

We are reminded, continuously, how various worries are: unpleasing breath, badly adjusted headlights, rheumatic trigger spots, unaverage children, insufficient control of the pelvic muscles, father changing the nappies badly, mother saying you can't have children and keep an orderly home, people dying unnecessarily of tetanus, and the intrusions of quarrelsome neighbours.

It is, however, a compassionate world, in which the worried help the worried. Elbow to elbow around a board-room table a pursed-lipped lady doctor, a tired parson, an angry-eyed, Joad-bearded magistrate and a bald, long-necked, long-headed psychologist worry at the worries of lesser mortals.

Mrs A. is worried because she has moved from a small town to an industrial neighbourhood, and her son, who had a nice way of speaking before, has acquired a slovenly accent; Mr B. because Mrs B. persistently flirts with the important business contacts whom he brings home for her to entertain; Mr and Mrs C. because their son, a 'wayward but likeable boy' of fifteen and a half, has started to take an interest in girls, and uses the telephone, without his parents' leave, to make appointments with them; Mrs D. because at the age of forty-two she is going to have another baby, and can't face going through it all again.

Their betters, for ever wiping or chewing or tapping their horn-rimmed glasses, puzzle out worldly-wise words of advice: 'He'll grow out of it, don't worry. . . . Sometimes you get two streams of motivation running together. . . All husbands and wives find it difficult to shine together . . . You should be much more worried if he *didn't* want to look at a girl.'

Next week, to make a change, we are gaily promised a sanitary inspector on household pests. A man in a hard collar, he treats us to worrying tales of rats spreading disease, spoiling the food and damaging the furniture; of insects feeding on human beings during the night. But he offers us remedies—a rodent operative, complete with 'knowhow' and 'gadgets'; a man in a mask spraying insecticide on our ants and cockroaches, boasting a fair measure of control but—a last stab of worry—not quite a hundred per cent.

For other worries other remedies. For the housewife, shopping parties in a borrowed car with Celia to Croydon, where the vegetables are 'awfully good', the price of tomatoes is 'pretty stabilized', there are plenty of cheap lettuces with 'good little hearts', pork chitterlings may be had from an old-fashioned butcher, and parsley is plentiful, which 'makes everything look prettier'.

For those worried by ignorance, a smart well-educated lady and gentleman, able to answer any questions: 'How did bubble and squeak get its name? What is a golliwog? How do you eat a pomegranate? How can I train my budgerigar to sit on my fingers? When will it start to talk? I am also blind. Does this worry the budgerigar?'

For all there are brief but blissful escapes into a world of fantasy: sunlit breaks, generously provided by advertisers, between the dark clouds of the everyday programmes. In a Disneyish world of animated freaks and dancing puppets, we relax to the prospect of Heavenly Nylons, the Latest in Lino, the Lilting Fragrance of Lavender, and Sleep that Knits Up the Ravelled Sleave of Care.

But the sovereign remedy for all the worries of the looking-glass world is neither lino nor nylons, lavender nor sleep, but Mr Godfrey Winn. This old-young man, with the dark worried rims around his eyes, is endowed with the even more beneficial power of transforming mortal lives. Arrayed in a halo of silvery hair, with a ring of boyish sincerity in his light, high voice, Mr Winn purveys the silver lining to every human cloud.

Seated at his desk, leaning on his elbows, he clasps and unclasps his hands as he confides to us the problems tormenting him. 'No one,' a lady has written to him, 'seems to think of me as a woman.' Mr Winn fades out and we see her, all smart at her work in a Bayswater store, a smart sales gentleman beside her not thinking of her as a woman.

Mr Winn fades in again, impulsively rises to his feet, stands poised before book-shelves of volumes finely bound, restlessly paces to and fro within the limits of the camera angle, his tie flopping out unheeded, then gracefully subsides, perching on the edge of the desk, puckering his forehead as the words of wisdom come tumbling out.

'D'ye know,' he says, lapsing for an unguarded moment into colloquial terms, 'there's one rule in life which always wins. *Know* yourself. *Be* yourself. That's what I wrote to her. Go to the staff dance. But not as a fashion silhouette. As a woman of flesh and blood. Now I'd like to show you this woman after she'd had this letter from me.'

She fades in again, unmistakably all flesh and blood, the smart sales gentleman now thinking of her as a woman and taking her down to supper. ('I never thought of you as human, but always wished you were.' 'I began to wonder whether I was myself.') Mr Winn, mastering a quiver in his voice, concludes, 'I think, don't you, that from now on she's going to be a *real person*.' Winn's Wisdom. It's a Tonic. It's a *Miracle*!

Mr Winn, in his Godhead, modestly does not claim 'omnipotence'. But his transformations are none the less striking. With the sensibility and compassion, if not of a Dickens, then of a Marie Corelli, he sees deep into the hungry, lonely souls of men and women alike. He is a man who has suffered. ('*I* knew what loneliness was when I first came to London as a boy of sixteen. But it's worse if you're a widow.') He spares himself no agonies of mind. ('All over the week-end, I've thought and *thought* about their problem. *Will* that home be happy?')

He is a man who has seen life. The grammar-school boy, ashamed of his posh friends knowing his dad's a commissionaire, is given as a parable the saying of the boy in Mr Winn's naval mess: 'My mum's the best cook in our street'. A small-boy half-smile plays over his lips, as he fades out on us till Thursday week: 'That's the way *any* son should speak of his mother.'

LORD KINROSS

'I take it you're in charge here?'

'What *a relief to get away from it all!*'

Bridge in Illyria

Scene: A hall.
Enter TRUMPIN *and his wife, the hosts:* BIDDUP *and his wife, the guests.*

TRUM.: Stand all apart. (*They do so.*) Cousins, we have decreed
    The time 'twixt supper and the earliest cock
    At cards shall be beguil'd.

ALL: It shall be done.

TRUM.: As tailors talk of points and ruffs, so we
    As gamesters will; let's talk of honour-tricks.

BID.: My mind mislikes me such a tricky honour.
    Who takes my tricks takes trash; but for my name—
    I am no boaster, yet I dare avouch
    There's none in Naples, Milan, Padua, no
    Nor where the Tiber rolls, that's held so high
    In spotless reputation. Bridge is such stuff
    As fame is made on; therefore, on this charge
    Cry: 'Bridge for glory, guineas, and St George!'

LADY T.: Devouring rats, dry rot, and ruthless Time
    Rend and deracinate our fairest cards.
    One pack alone is left; 'tis in the closet.

TRUM. (*shouting*): What, Lucius, ho!

Enter a tottering and toothless SERVANT

SERV.:   What would my gracious master?

TRUM.: Bring me the merry pasteboards, freak'd with aces
    And crownèd kings and queens, whose red and black
    Nature's own sweet and cunning hand laid on,
    Mass'd in their suits and index-pip'd withal——
    Cards, sirrah! Gap'st thou, knave?

SERV.:   My liege, I go,
    Swifter than Hector to assail the foe.

                     [*Exit very slowly.*

BID.: What bloody man is that?

LADY T.:   That is the servant,
    Raw in the tooth and brutish in's aspect,
    Yet fill'd with kindness and compassion.
    Good Mistress Biddup, spread yourself awhile.

LADY B.: Mass, neighbour Trumpin, I were fain to stand,
    My capon to digest, my tongue to loose.
    For though I have no gift of eloquence,
    Methinks I am a prophet new inspir'd.
    Come all you justicers of day and night,
    Drench us in slams, finesses, forcing bids,
    Squeeze plays, preparèd clubs, Blackwood responses——

BID.: Peace, prattling shrew; to a nunnery, get thee hence!

TRUM.: What noise without?

LADY T.:   It was the nightingale
    Full featly furnish'd for his amorous art.

TRUM.: Play, music. (*Music heard.*) Welkin, ring!
    Enough, no more. (*Music stops.*)
    'Tis not so sweet now as it was before.

LADY B.: Marry, Sir Tumpin, 'twas a tuneful strain.
    (*Aside*) I had as lief my grandam's bitch should howl.

Re-enter SERVANT *with pack of cards of tray.*

TRUM.: Give me the pack. Where are the scoring blocks?

SERV.: No block is to be found, my noble lord.

TRUM.: A block for thine head, thou block-headed ape!
    Out, dog; a murrain gripe thee!

SERV.:   Sir, good night.
    I to the pantry will retire anon
    And drown my griefs in sack and patience.
    (*Aside*) Be still, my tongue; they must not know that I
    The banish'd duke am.
          (*Aloud*) Lucius takes his leave.   [*Exit.*

TRUM.: Now let us pair.

BID.:   Say pair again, that thus
    We may repair our loves.

(*All laugh. But the cut shows that husbands and wives are partners. All look depressed.*)

TRUM. (*aside*):   O deadly strife
    When husband cutteth partner to his wife!

BID. (*to his wife*):
    Will 't please you back the arras, sweetest chuck?
    I my backside against the glowing embers
    Will roast amain; not otherwise than when
    Apollo in his car bestrides the heavens
    High in the burnish'd noonday. Prithee, shuffle.

(*During the next speeches* TRUMPIN, *on the left of* BIDDUP, *shuffles, and his wife cuts to* BIDDUP, *who deals.*)

LADY T.: The quality of cards is not the best.
    They stick like syrup to the fingers' ends,
    Or as the serried wasps in rank September
    Around the jam-pot festering. Doth it content ye,
    A groat a point?

LADY B.:   A hundred points a ducat.

TRUM.: Why, that were just, go to.

ALL: Ay, even so.

LADY T. (*singing*):
    Heigh ho, the mistletoe,
    Heigh, jolly Robin, and the nut-brown ale.
    For your snail, sir, he carries his house on's head;

you cannot keep him out of your herbaceous border. This remark was formerly out of favour, save on Collop Monday.

BID. (*aside*):

To bid, or not to bid, that is the question:
Whether 'twere wiser for one round to pass,
Or to take action with this string of diamonds,
And, by pre-empting, fool them. To bid—to pass—
Ay, there's the rub; for should I bid my hour,
Jove nor the Delphic Oracle can proclaim
What lies in Fortune's palm. In passing then——

LADY B.: Lorenzo, come, we wait upon your bid.

BID.: I dream. I cry you mercy. Well, Three Diamonds.

TRUM.: Three Diamonds, quotha! Double, on my life!

LADY B.: No bid.

LADY T.:   Three Spades,

BID.:   Four diamonds,

TRUM.:   'Sdeath, Four Spades!

LADY B. (*aside*):

I doubt my spouse's temper; in good sooth,
Raise I him not to game, sure he'll mar all.
O Atropos! O Jupiter! O crikey!
Was his call genuine or just a psyche?
Is this a diamond which I see before me?
Not one i' the whole collection; this my hand
Is full of blackness as an Æthiop's curls.
How shall I judge? Here's yet some red support.
(*Aloud*) Five Diamonds.

LADY T.:   Nay.

BID.:   No more,

TRUM.:   My bolt is shot,

My course is run; and as the noisome hippo,
Track'd to his lair in steaming Afric swamp,

Perforce himself submergeth, lo! I pass.
(TRUMPIN *leads and* LADY BIDDUP *lays down dummy*.)

LADY B.: I have no joy of this contract to-night.
It is too rash, too unadvis'd, too sudden.

BID.: Vipers and toads!

LADY T.:   What ails our worthy neighbour?

BID.: Detested dummy! O thou spawn of hell,
Rear'd in the slime of Tartarus his lake!
What diamonds, patch? What trumps, thou cream-fac'd loon?

LADY B.: Husband, avoid!

BID.:   Avoid, by Culbertson!
A void in trumps, no diamonds in thy hand;
These bloody things are hearts! I am undone.

TRUM.: Sweet friends, be patient yet.

BID.:   Out, palsied dolt!
Now, by my grandsire's beard, my blood grows hot.
Grand slam in clubs shall pay for this
(*Seizes a club and strikes his wife.*). Take that!

LADY B.: O, I am vulnerable. (*Dies.*)

LADY T.: Rash and unhappy man, now look what thou hast done.

BID.: Bianca, Bianca, stay a little. What,
Too late? I follow thee. Vain world, adieu!
My heart is now unguarded. (*Stabs himself.*)
Peace is made
So give us burial with a single spade. (*Dies.*)

TRUM.: (*to the audience*):

'Tis but a game; success is little worth.
What is to come will come and coming comes
As it had come a hundred times before.
Ripeness is all. Go, bid the soldiers shoot!

CURTAIN

ALAN PHILLIPS

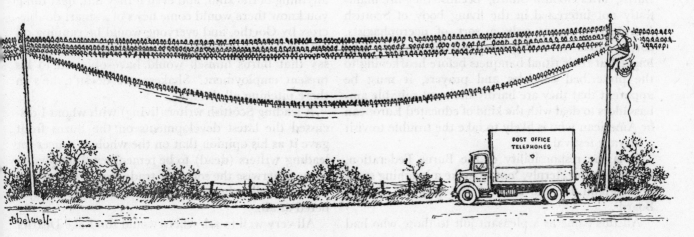

Homer Nodded Here

EXHIBITIONS of rage are at almost all times welcome and pleasant, and when they occur in accordance with custom and hallowed tradition, especially so. Which is where Sydney Goodsir Smith, poet, has done the right thing. What he is in a rage about is the thing he thinks, rightly or wrongly, is happening to the poet Burns.

As is universally known, once a year in January people all over the Universe meet to honour the memory and recall the achievement of Burns. This happens anyway, but it is normally expected that at some date decently in advance of these celebrations someone should exclaim, denounce, and declare with ill-disguised disgust that the memory of Burns is being exploited, commercialized, dragged at the chariot wheels of this or that.

This year this opening part of the ceremony was left unusually, even, some thought, dangerously late. There were those who feared that yet one more time-honoured etc., etc., was going down the drain.

The alarm was unjustified. Sydney Goodsir Smith had the matter in hand. His rage came up in plenty of time and was only waiting for the winter issue of the *Saltire Review* to be put in action. It was an especially high-class rage because it wasn't just about the ordinary annual celebrations but about the super-one planned for 1959 to mark the bi-centenary of Burns' birth, which, many hope, will send the hard-currency customers whizzing north so fast that Strat-ford-on-Avon will appear as a mere blur, and knock the Irish Tourist Board for six.

'Because the Burns Federation have mummified Burns,' cries Goodsir Smith, 'because they are manifestly not interested in the living body of Scottish literature, but are only a sort of necrophagists, corpse-eaters devouring the symbolic cadaver [the haggis] at their ritual banquets before hearkening to the prescribed canticles and prayers, it must be apparent that they are hardly the most suitable ambassadors to deal with the kind of educated European or American who is likely to take the trouble to visit a literary festival.'

It is the responsibility of the Burns Federation, says Mr Smith sternly, 'not to make a laughing stock of Scotland for the sake of the Scottish Tourist Board'.

All this came as a pleasant jolt to those who had forgotten about a haggis being a symbolic cadaver, and in addition Goodsir Smith sweetened the atmosphere by pointing out, in a spirit of fair play and considered judgment, that 'Of course we are not unique; England has its Stratford-on-Avon, which is a more vulgar display of unashamed daylight robbery than anything in Scotland.'

The number of men who are prepared to state in public that they are positively in favour of vulgar display, unashamed daylight robbery and necrophagy is small, and it was to be expected that a majority would devote a couple of minutes of their time to saying, 'Absolutely,' 'It's a scandal,' and 'Take that poet out of your mouth at once,' before returning to the job of seeing how far Burns can be tapped for a further posthumous contribution to the hotel business.

On second thoughts, a good many good men in Edinburgh were saying this week that after all there seems no compelling reason to let poets, saints, etc., off this type of contribution, which would appear to be a rather painless kind of tax so far as they are concerned.

If there were any likelihood of some international agreement under which the saints and singers would all get out of the Tourist industry at the same time, and stay out of it for a couple of years, that might be a solution. Were Shakespeare and St Patrick, for example, to stand down, it would be reasonable to ask Burns to do the same.

But nobody acquainted with the facts supposes that either of the first two named are likely to do anything of the kind, and even if they did, next thing you know there would come news of a smart double-cross by Goethe, and everyone would be running off with their dollars to Weimar. And who on earth is to say that Burns himself would have objected to his present employment? Shakespeare doesn't, he's in there pitching all the time.

A leading Scottish writer (living) with whom I discussed the latest developments on the Burns front gave it as his opinion that on the whole it's nicer for leading writers (dead) to be remembered simply because otherwise the souvenir trade would slump and many boarding-houses close, than not to be remembered at all.

All very well to ask where would the Lake District

be without Wordsworth, but where, one may also inquire, would Wordsworth be without the Lake District publicity men to keep him going? Way down among the Brownings, as like as not.

Before there were motor-coaches to take people to Freshwater, Isle of Wight, hardly anyone had heard of Tennyson for years, and a year or so after the death of Dylan Thomas people started going to Wales. So far from doing harm to poets, this sort of thing does them a bit of good.

Goodsir Smith should possibly think back to the time, not of so very yore, when nobody noticed poets and others of the writin' and paintin' set simply because nobody could see what possible use they were, and you got familiar situations like King George's remark to Gibbon about scribble, scribble, scribble eh? True, you also had a writer here and there trying to look useful, claiming big practical effectiveness, such as the song-writer who said, 'Let who will write a nation's laws, so I may write its songs,' but very few took him seriously, and still devoted their main time and money to trying to nobble M.P.s and senior Civil Servants.

There were a few jobs where a poet or someone of that kind could do a useful stint, as, for instance, writing 'Rule, Britannia!' but by and large it was Tourism which sent poets' stock up to where it stands to-day, because it was only Tourism which showed how handy a high-grade, properly attested poet can come in. All I can say to Goodsir Smith is: If this be necrophagy, make the most of it.

CLAUD COCKBURN

'Do you suppose it's part of it—or should we tell him?'

'Is it A.C. or D.C.?'

smilby.

'Have you the same thing in C sharp?'

Television Man

THROUGH no fault of his own (for he seemed of good character, albeit with some tendency to shiftlessness) this young man had been forced into the pursuit or calling of Television Man. His own word for it was 'the Announcing Lark,' and after overcoming his suspicion that I might be connected with the Inland Revenue he answered my questions readily enough. He was sturdily built, the only signs of privation being his pallor and a slight stooping of the shoulders. His suit was of some dark material, neatly pressed but shiny at the revers and on the sleeves. He had on clean linen, and wore the tie of some Club or Regiment; he could not remember which, although I pressed him hard for the information. Altogether he presented an appearance at once sober, earnest, and apprehensive.

'Why, bless you, sir, there must be upwards of thirty of us playing the "announcing lark" in London at this time, and maybe more; indeed it's hard to tell, it not being a *settled* profession as you might say of bricklaying, or the selling of roasted chestnuts, or the like. No, sir, my father was not in the same line, for in his time such a thing was hardly thought of, nor did many see the possibility of living by such a fanciful occupation, not in those days. He did well as a grocer in the North, and I was to follow him. But the hours being so long, and the labour so arduous, I was not inclined to continue at it. Yes, I fought in the wars, and was a fair enough hand at it, I dare say, and gave as good as I got. [He had served in the Royal Air Force.] After that I suppose I fell in with evil companions, who put it in my mind to seek out some occupation where the pickings were O.K. [that is, the remuneration was satisfactory] and the work but little. At that time many were taking to the theatrical life, for in the wars the public had paid to see anything, however uncouthly presented, and there was ample scope still for a presentable gent who could get a part by heart and possessed more than one suit. All that is changing now, for the public seek other attractions, or, if they *are* to see a play, all must be nicely done, and with proper entertainers that have been at pains to take lessons.

'Yes, I fell in with the theatricals, and did well enough for a time up and down the country. But, the work being so strenuous, I resolved to make my way to London and find some more congenial branch of the "lark"; for I had heard that there was much to be picked up [earned] by way of appearing at the Palladium, etc., or by turning agent and working the best fiddle of all [engaging in the most profitable vocation].'

He went on to give an account of the trials which beset him in the metropolis: how he lived on friends, took engagements as scullion, 'carried a spear' for Mr Donald W——, and finally, having had an almost new suit sent to him by his father, fell to 'televisioning'.

'Oh, they seemed happy enough to have me, for I had taught myself a proper way of speaking, and could smile or look solemn according as to how it was required. Yes, I like it well enough, I dare say. The way of it is this, you see: suppose there is to be some piece of ribaldry played before the cameras, or some learned discourse, or it may be a lady to pretend to sing, with some fetching division arranged between the one breast and the other so that she may seem the more accomplished; why, then, I will first appear and will state the names of the personages concerned. If it is to be a comical personage, why then I will save his name to the *end* of my pronouncement, and say it right loudly, and as though on the point of laughing. That is a "dodge" we have. Or if it is to be a weighty matter, then I will frown; and in this way prepare the public for what is to follow.

'Yes, there is skill in it, as you remark. Then there are other "dodges". [This I took to mean 'tricks-of-the-trade,' or 'subtleties'.] One is, to appear to have a cold, and apologize for being husky: then the public will send many a score of bottles of rum, which fetch a tidy amount if sold at half-price. Oh, yes, the public is generous to such unfortunates as we, upon the smallest encouragement. Another "dodge" is to make out to be a "personality", as by yawning at the camera, or biting your nails, or combing your hair: any little thing to set you apart from other men. By this you may soon be chosen for "acting" for the moving pictures, and so make a good match. Talent? Why, I suppose that comes after.

'No, I do not complain, for I have brought myself to these straits. I might have had my own car by now if I had applied myself to my father's trade. But I make the best of things, and trust in Equity. I share this four-roomed apartment with another even worse placed than myself, and we do middling well. Yes, I have meat twice a week, or three times if the weather is cold. At other times I have mostly spaghetti. I must provide my own clothes, and keep myself tidy on all occasions. [He was unwilling to divulge his weekly stipend, as are many of his class, but insisted, on my cross-examining him, that it wasn't enough. I believe he was frank and trustworthy in most of his statements.] When I have paid my rent, and bought the necessities, I have barely enough to see all the moving-pictures which take my fancy. But my "girl-friend" is "well-heeled," and proud to be seen about with me.'

Upon being questioned as to his thoughts of the future he replied: 'Why, I should be content if I could only get into the "Interviewing Lark," for there one meets a variety of people, and so has opportunities for advancement. Ah, if only I could master as many "dodges" as Mr Richard D——! [Here he sighed.] Then I should think myself fortunate indeed, to be mentioned in the same breath as Royalty. But that's a dream.'

Before I took my leave he confided that he did have one ambition: it was, he said, to find some 'lark' which carried an expense account. In this, I may say, he resembled many another member of the growing army of London's poor.

ALEX ATKINSON

'Would you wrap it as a gift?'

'Testing, 1 – 2 – 3. Testing——'

The Lush Life

THE *Sunday Express*, of course, is perfectly right. Recently, denouncing the lush lives of lawyers, it pilloried four or five leading Q.C.s who are, it seems, in shameful receipt of incomes to which no human beings, with the possible exception of crooners and obviously of newspaper proprietors, are entitled. Lawyers, it must be admitted, have it too lush. It is now possible, without the aid of leaks from the Bar Council, to give personal details of other lush lives among the legal profession—men for whom two-figure cheques are an almost annual occurrence and who may, even as this is written, be sitting down to celebrate with half a bottle of Australian Burgundy in luxury apartments off the Finchley Road.

Take, if you can bear to, Peskett. It is certainly time Peskett was exposed. He is now about twenty-nine and was called to the Bar before the profession had been advertised as the softest racket of them all. Looking at the procession of judges passing through the Law Courts at the start of his first term, seeing the Q.C.s strolling behind them in pairs, chattering to each other, gently teasing Miss Rose Heilbron, he may almost have been fired with longing for a civilized and even occasionally useful life. This, rather than the immediate prospect of £40,000 a year, may have led him to struggle through his examinations, with the help of a number of slim books with titles like *Potted Torts in a Nutshell* and a liverish tutor in Chancery Lane who specializes in

making English Law clear to the subtle minds of Indian students. Once called to the Bar, however, Peskett was naturally after the loot and therefore had to enter chambers. It is known to be impossible to operate as a lush lawyer from a bed-sitting-room in Chelsea or any sort of temporary booth erected on the pavement in the Strand. Chambers are essential, and to obtain the entrée to one of these select establishments Peskett offered himself and the sum of fifty guineas to become a pupil for six months.

The first chambers he went to specialized in pupils. At the top of a remote staircase, up which no solicitor had climbed for a large number of years, sat an ancient clerk who welcomed Peskett with the flickered smile of an elderly toad putting out his tongue to catch a fly. He was taken in to see the head of the chambers, an old man who sat at a desk one leg of which was supported by three volumes of *Haggard's Ecclesiastical Reports*, wearing a green eye-shield and reading the obituaries in *The Times*. Around him in the gloaming sat the other pupils, a retired major who became interested in law after a court-martial in Gibraltar, a lady in glass beads who was studying to conduct her own case before a rent tribunal, and a former income tax inspector who resolved to go to the Bar after winning a modest pittance on the treble chance. On the mantelpiece, gathering soot, sat a single brief, a relic of the rush of divorce cases which were a symptom of the moral lapse immediately after

if it did Peskett would find himself last in line after the débutante, he moved to his present chambers. There he shares a small room, about three foot by five, with two men of his own age and a retired Iraqi Judge who luckily, for he is a bulky man, never comes in. He has finished his pupillage, and now has a practice of his own. His fee is frequently three guineas, for which he usually travels at least once to a remote Magistrates' Court before the case is reached and then twice more because there never seems to be time to hear all Peskett's cases in one day. Once, when the head of his chambers caught cold, Peskett took over a fifty-guinea brief which so turned his head with success that he got married. At least in time for the christening of his second child the fifty guineas is liable to be paid. He discusses all his cases with his

the 1914 war. Apparently it had been delivered to that set of chambers by mistake and never taken away.

As one vintage brief seemed a small quantity of work for so many pupils to share, Peskett next went to the chambers of a fashionable leader. There he found five very young old Etonians all in Edwardian suits playing cricket in the passage outside the clerks' room, their wicket being kept by the startlingly beautiful débutante daughter of a County Court judge, a girl who looked, on the days when she sat listening in Court, wistfully appealing in a winged collar. As the leader's practice seemed unlikely to devolve on any of these sporting pupils, and as even

wife, does a lot of work as a poor man's lawyer for nothing, and reads, at weekends, plaintive letters from his bank manager about the unfortunate results of the Government's economic policy. He is, in a curious way, not discontented.

Peskett, it may be said, is not typical. He hasn't really got established in the butter and egg existence of the Bar. Look, then, at two other capitalists, Hampton and Fender-Jones. Hampton, at sixty-four, has a good junior practice on the Western circuit. It is quite true that he spends most of his weekends on the train to or from Weston-super-Mare, which makes him rather tired. It is also true that when he defends a murderer at Bodmin, which he does extremely well, his fee from the State doesn't quite cover the cost of his hotel and leaves him slightly out of pocket on his railway fare. Extravagantly having sent his three sons to public schools, he has spent most of the lush fees he ever had and, without a pension, looks forward to working until, changing at Bristol very late one night, he drops dead. Curiously enough his three sons have all got jobs in the City where, on their short journeys to the West End, they eat on expense accounts and retire at fifty-one.

Finally, for a man at the top, take Fender-Jones. Painstaking and thorough, he was so over-worked at the Junior Bar that, late in middle age, he posted an exhausted application to the Lord Chancellor for Silk. The Lord Chancellor, a malignant fairy, granted this foolish request. Fender-Jones bought a full-bottomed wig and, for some reason he can never understand, his clients vanished like shadows from the day he put it on. He has now been for years quite unoccupied. He comes into his chambers every day and is always ready to discuss anyone else's cases or help them by looking up the law. Every day he has lunch with the benchers of his Inn. Tactfully they never ask him about his practice. He has taken to drinking Cyprus wine instead of port after dinner; he hopes that if he drinks enough of it it may do him in before his small capital is exhausted.

Well, there you are—Peskett, Hampton and Fender-Jones. If they read this article they may feel ashamed of living so well out of a job they find, in spite of everything, has an endless and ever-changing fascination. Or they may, more wisely, decide to give it all up for a lush life on the *Sunday Express*.

GEOFFREY LINCOLN

'Isn't that our waiter?'

'We'll have to stop meeting like this. My insurance company's getting suspicious.'

'It's been doing that for ages. . .'

The Public v. The Public

'Mr Frank Powell, Clerkenwell magistrate, described as "Gilbertian" a situation in which, if he imposed fines on summonses brought for the public benefit against a nationalized undertaking, the public would have to pay the fine.'—Daily Telegraph

I AM lying awake with a dismal headache, and repose is taboo'd by anxiety,
    For a Public Concern, I am sorry to learn, has inflicted a wrong on society;
Such a clear case of tort must be taken to court, and I trust that all true men and women'll
Entirely agree that the Public should be in the dock as the dastardly criminal.
I shall not be resigned until someone is fined for a deed so revoltingly shameless,
And I speak, I may add, for the Public, by gad, whose behaviour throughout has been blameless;
And I hope judge and jury will bridle their fury and act with judicial restraint if
They find each contendent is both the defendant and also, *per contra*, the plaintiff.

E. V. MILNER

Dancing Gaiters

Sunlight blessed the Convocation of Canterbury. It set the gaiters dancing across Lambeth Bridge, blended purple cassocks in an impressionist fantasy with roses and delphiniums in the Archbishop's flowerbeds, glanced through the tall gothic windows of his library on the gleaming silver or gold of pectoral crosses.

'Please do not touch the books,' said a notice above the Archbishop's head. 'But what are they for?' asked the Bishop of Exeter, plaintively. Perhaps simply to delight the eye by their rich and mellow bindings, the ear by the alliterative litany of their alphabetical order: Featley's *Clavis Mystica*, Fenner's *Works*, Fiddes' *Discourses*, Fleetwood's *Sermons*, Hall's *Meditations and Vowes*, Hall's *Treatises*, Heylin's *Tracts* . . .

Before assembling at Lambeth, members of Convocation had attended a service at St Paul's, part of the order of which read:

The Royal Writ for summoning the Convocation and the Certificate of the execution of His Grace's Mandate . . . will be read.

The Registrar will præconize the members of the Upper House.

The Registrar will then read the Schedule of Contumacy.

The President will then admonish, in Latin, the Clergy to form themselves into a Lower House . . .

Having been writted, certified, præconized, scheduled against contumacy, and admonished in Latin, those present were sufficiently chastened to accept the quaint old designation, 'the inferior clergy'.

There must have been a good deal of dusting of old Latin grammars and dictionaries. Not only was the St Paul's service, including the sermon, in Latin:

each day's business at Lambeth opened with half the Prayer-book litany in Latin (which one zealous young reporter began to try to take down in shorthand). The first half was read by the new Bishop of Oxford, the second by the Archdeacon of Taunton, newly-elected Prolocutor of the Lower House. The sonorous cadences flowed smoothly enough from the tongues of both, though the Prolocutor had some difficulty with the unpalatable word *fidissimisque*. The pronunciation used was a seemly Anglican compromise between the 'old' and the 'new': 'continental' vowel-sounds, but none of those Italianate 'chees and chaws.'

Dr Fisher is a truly superb chairman—the essence of the art being to jolly everyone along so that there is unanimous agreement with the chairman's own view in the shortest possible time. He is never pompous: again and again he let slip such observations as 'Then there's a tiny committee—I forget just what it's for', and 'Is there really any point in passing this resolution?'

He is in a sense—to use a Parliamentary analogy—Speaker and Prime Minister in one; and he gives Convocation far stronger guidance than Parliament as a whole would take from any Government. He said that the decision on the Church of South India ought not to be delayed because he had indicated to other provinces of the Anglican Communion that they would know the mind of the Church of England about it in May, and they had already been waiting for two months. Parliament would have resented being pressed by such an argument on an important issue of principle. Convocation did not resent it, no doubt because clergymen are holier and humbler than M.P.s.

Contrasts and comparisons with Parliament were irresistible—and Convocation came well out of many of them. Canon Smethurst—very much a key man—was unfortunately suffering from a fractured jaw. Perhaps the plaster he wore served as a symbolic warning against pride of oratory: at any rate, the speeches were in general briefer, less rhetorical, and freer from gesture than those of M.P.s.

As in Parliament or any other dignified assembly, mildly comic remarks or incidents excited disproportionate mirth. Bishop Sinker drew an appreciative roar of laughter when—after many others had spoken on South India—he opened: 'I feel some diffidence in speaking about the Church of South India as I have not been there for fully eighteen months.' For some reason, again, the House was convulsed by the announcement that a return ticket to Canterbury had been found in the robing-room.

Wit was taken as well as humour. The Reverend

thelwell.

Michael Bruce remarked of the credal orthodoxy of the Church of South India: 'I have no doubt that if you rooted around there you would find a certain number of heretics—perhaps as high a proportion as in the Church of England.' The Archbishop pungently regretted an amendment by the Lower House depriving the Duke of Edinburgh of the epithet 'versatile' in the Loyal Address. 'It was the only word,' he said, 'which gave any human or relevant tone to the whole document. However, their Lordships are happy to accept the united advice of the Lower House'—happy, it was ironically implied, that the document was now inhuman, irrelevant, and utterly correct.

It was almost the only point in the whole two and a half days which the Archbishop had to yield. The only faint hint of the sort of clash familiar in the Commons—between 'the machine' and the back benches —came when Archbishop and Prolocutor repeatedly asked that names of those wishing to speak should be sent in in advance. The Reverend H. Riley complained that this was a 'new procedure' which would tend to make the debate more rigid. As Mr Speaker might have, the Prolocutor assured him that this was only intended to make the debate better balanced, to facilitate not to limit it.

But there was such unanimity on the main issue, among so many succeeding speakers, that the debate resembled one of those Commons debates on foreign affairs in which few speeches disturb the atmosphere of bipartisanism.

The proposition that the Church of England should gradually enter into closer relations with the Church of South India was, indeed, universally acceptable, with some difference of emphasis only on the tempo of the process—the Evangelical foot being on the accelerator, the Anglo-Catholic foot on the brake. Surprisingly, perhaps, the vehicle still seems to move, in the stately cautious progress historically appropriate to *Ecclesia Anglicana*.

Bishops and parsons *en masse* are an easy target for the comedian or satirist. But the abiding impression of those three days is of men singularly free from rancour, sincere men, humbly confident that the spirit of God was moving among them.

TOM DRIBERG

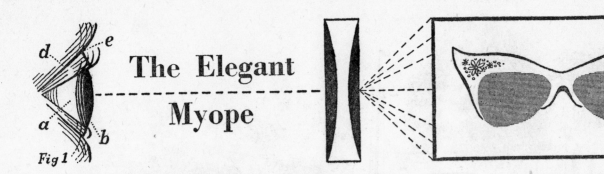

Fig 1

The Elegant Myope

THIS season, spectacles can be just as silly as hats, and that is saying something. The elegant myope who needs to wear glasses all the time does not make a virtue out of her necessity, she makes a vanity of it. In the delicate art of putting oneself over, spectacles have become a very important accessory.

Men, of course, have always made use of them in the architecture of character-building. In China they were regarded as a symbol of wisdom, a mark of degree; many a wise, clear-sighted mandarin had plain glass in his great round bamboo frames. Leather framed spectacles tied to the ears with strings were the sign of a man of substance in seventeenth-century Spain. In more modern times, in the nineteen-twenties, no American who wished 'to win friends and influence people' could afford to be without horn-rimmed glasses, however keen his sight. Horn-rims did to the meaningless face what beards do to receding chins; in a world of dominoes, it was the double-blanks who wore the thickest, boldest rims.

Feminine vanity, on the other hand, does not lie so much in trying to impress with prosperity and success as to bowl over with beauty, grace, and

charm. There are no early records of women wearing spectacles. Through the centuries ladies have worked in dim-lit castles at their interminable tapestries, in country houses at their unnecessary needlework and still less necessary water-colours, all without benefit of glasses. No urban society lady would admit to any weakness of sight. While men of fashion found the quizzer and the spy-glass telling elegancies, all that the lady of fashion could have was a little spy-glass hidden in her fan, or a magnifying glass in her scent bottle. Lorgnettes for ladies came later, for elderly ladies only.

Sun-glasses were the first spectacles to become accessories to the feminine mode. This was when it became the thing to go to the French Riviera in the dazzling summer instead of, as before, only in the paler sunshine of the winter months. Dark glasses, through this association, came to give an air of continental chic and idle richness. But to understand just why dark glasses aid attractiveness whereas clear glasses are a handicap to be overcome, it is necessary to recall the masked face at a ball: it is the mystery behind the mask, it is the glamour behind the dark lenses. For the wearer, it is also the sensation of being able to gaze unabashed, of being gazed at unembarrassed; it is boldness with the blinds drawn.

Everyday spectacles are just as highly-charged as sun-glasses: shaped as swans, trimmed with love-birds, some with earrings hanging from their side-pieces, the day of decadence is at hand. Upswept, harlequin, grasshopper, elfin . . . is it not time to call a halt? Time, indeed, to cry mercy! Yet the cumulative effect is such that even she who most genuinely wishes to contract out of the glamour game begins to feel dissatisfied with her exciting glasses. They look old-fashioned, they smack of National Health. A new pair, she thinks, would do more for her than a new hat; her new hat will do nothing for her without new glasses. She may prefer the new wavy side-pieces which are less severe than ordinary straight legs. If she wishes she can have glasses designed to her hair-style, or a hair-style designed to her glasses. She must,

ff

there's no help for it, have several different pairs for different social occasions.

For evening, spectacles have turned into conversation pieces. Studded with coloured stones or diamanté, the best are the work of jewellers' craftsmen and can be matched to earrings and necklace. Diamanté clip-lorgnettes, however, have the greatest evening elegance, entirely free from the taint of necessity. These fold in two to form a dress clip, the back of the clip being the handle of the lorgnette. Less expensive folding lorgnettes are made in tortoiseshell, and sometimes coloured plastics. So modish, indeed, have lorgnettes become that one optician is extending the vogue still further back and introducing copies of eighteenth-century spy-glasses: first-rate accessories for First Nights.

Lorgnette gestures, carefully studied, can be effectively employed with spectacles proper; and an aid to such pretty by-play is the 'Speclet' chain. This is a gilt chain which clips to the end of each side-piece and goes round the back of the neck. Primarily for public speakers who need spectacles for glancing at their notes, it is quite a thing for anyone who frequently takes her glasses off and on: and everyone *should*. For the art of wearing spectacles effectively, femininely, is not to let them be a static feature of the face. Taken off and on, swung on the hand, used for the pensive stroking of the chin, the absent-minded tapping of the teeth, the doodle on the table-cloth, spectacles are an instrument of flirtation as was the Edwardian fan. Only imagine! When sitting *tête-à-tête* there is the playful tap on the partner's shirt-front with the dainty jewel-studded glasses . . . followed by a blushing retreat behind the lenses till the music starts again.

ALISON ADBURGHAM

Cancel that trip Now

WHEN, in the late nineteen-twenties, Mr and Mrs Sidney Webb, in the interests of goodwill and understanding, went to visit Leon Trotsky in his first exile on the island of Prinkipo they wanted to talk to him about Fabianism and gradualness. They thought this personal contact would help make everything clear to him. Trotsky, for his part, was glad to have an opportunity to tell them, face to face, that they had their money on the wrong horse. He ranted lengthily about the absolute inevitability of bloody revolution in Britain; lamp-posts, barricades and all the rest of it.

'And what,' somebody asked Mrs Webb afterwards in London, 'did you say?'

'We told him "No",' said Mrs Webb.

Just another example of there not being as much gained by going to see people as people think. A very fervid believer in this notion of the beneficial get-together was Presbyterian Scottish Judge Lord Hernand, who thought that if the Pope would come to Edinburgh and drink a lot of claret with him the Pope would become a Protestant too. (He reasoned, according to a contemporary, that all men, including His Holiness, are basically good, and that since a lot of good claret brings their best qualities to the surface, a meeting of this kind would do the trick.) Lord Hernand was never disillusioned, because the Pope never turned up, but it seems pretty safe to assert that even if he had, nothing very constructive would have come of it.

Despite a long series of more or less catastrophic misunderstandings arising from get-togethers of one kind and another, people went right ahead thinking they would do good, as when, early in World War II, some genius said a whole lot would be gained if the late H. G. Wells went on an American tour and made personal contact with influential ex-President Hoover —might be a turning point in Anglo-American relations.

Wells trekked out to Palo Alto where Hoover was, and he sat down opposite Hoover and he talked. In his high voice he talked and he talked. Talked about civilization, menaces to it and ways of averting them, necessity for mutual understanding in the face of perils than which, etc. It was disconcerting, Mr Wells told me a long time later, because all this time Hoover's rather big face did not show so much as a flicker of interest round the edges. Still, understanding must be achieved, and Wells kept on and on, pulling out all the stops. When he had been talking without cessation for nearly twenty-five minutes, Hoover, immobile as a statue all this time, suddenly moved. He took a watch out of his waistcoat pocket and looked at it.

'I'm afraid,' he said, 'you'll have to excuse me. I have an appointment at this time with a Mr H. G. Wells.'

Probably top-ranking diplomats and Heads of State get some sort of immunization so that they can meet without getting maddened to the point of secretly planning a declaration of war by the way this fellow keeps getting little bits of cigarette tobacco on the tip of his tongue, and if he tells that story about the Irishman in Berlin just once more we break off diplomatic relations here and now.

For everyone else it's most fearfully dangerous, and no thinking person can see a Goodwill Mission setting out for anywhere without his heart in his mouth.

This is where the Russians were so tremendously clever during the war, staying away over there fighting the battle of Stalingrad and being loved and admired by all, while Texans and such had to come over here and be the butt of jokes about their accents and the size of their bankrolls, and even when the authorities got out little educational films showing them how to drink warm beer and play darts without offending a man from Croydon who was really quite a character—well, think of Dickens—everyone knew it didn't fully meet the case.

With barriers to international intercourse being freely lifted on all sides, it looks as though we may be on the verge of a period of international friction more embittered than anything seen since the steamed cabbage *v.* frog series of mutual recriminations first hashed up mutual esteem between the French and the English. Hardly anyone, including the Chinese and the Argentines, really likes foreigners, but just so long as they don't get too close they can at least pretend to. Then some reckless maniac makes up a party of tourists, and for everyone who comes back writing to the papers saying he met everywhere with unfailing kindness and courtesy and why can't British railway porters be the same, nine others have been gypped and insulted, and when we pointed out that it was a gross overcharge the man had never heard of the Battle of Britain and you'd have thought his lot had won the war.

There's been a lot of so-called expert flim-flam about that break there was until recently between Tito and the Russians, and now that there isn't a break any more people are flim-flamming more than ever about why it happened in the first place—stuff about Stalin and trends in the Kremlin and such. This is all so much hot air. The reason was get-togethers—goodwill tours and trade missions and all that. I was there; I saw it happen. It all started when we were motoring through the mountains of Montenegro with an official from the Yugoslav Foreign Office, and a man from the Swiss Red Cross, and a Russian trade representative who was going to export or import wine, I forget which.

As of 9 a.m., when we all met, goodwill was nearly overpowering. The Swiss loved and admired the Russian and the Yugoslav, and they loved him because he was there to help, and they quite liked me too, on account of not being a black-hearted reactionary like so many British one could mention.

When it began to rain the Swiss put on a pair of spectacles which had tiny little electrically-operated windscreen wipers on them, and the Yugoslav passed the remark that if the Yugoslav guerrillas and partisans had been so effete that they could not stand a little mountain rain without having elaborate gadgets of that kind to protect them, the outcome of the war would have been very different. No wonder, he mused, that the Swiss had remained neutral. The Swiss said he did hope it would not be very long before the Yugoslavs, who, he had always heard, were quite hard-working, managed to attain a level of technical and industrial efficiency somewhere near that of Switzerland. They might even, by that time, construct some good roads.

Meantime the Russian, who was peering out of the car at a village we happened to be passing through, sighed and kept shaking his head and said when he thought of the devastations that had occurred in Russia it was astonishing to see a village so little damaged in the war—it just showed what an easy war the Yugoslavs had had compared to the Russians. The Yugoslav was still yelling statistics at him when we reached another village which had been reduced, by bombing, gunfire and arson, to a series of piles of rubble.

'There,' shouted the Yugoslav, 'look at that! Is that a result of an easy war?'

The Russian looked out carefully at the rubble and said that naturally in Russia, where everyone worked enthusiastically and with high technical efficiency to repair the ravages wrought by the invaders, such a village would by now have been completely reconstructed. A pile of rubble like that would be considered a disgrace, proof of slackness or sabotage somewhere.

By now the noise was deafening, and I considered

AUTO·WAYS

SEE EUROPE IN ARMCHAIR COMFORT

LONDON – LISBON

Smilby.

Eric Burgin

'You've forgotten to kiss me good-bye. . .'

it my international duty to intervene with calm words of reason, everyone had done splendidly, different countries, different methods and so on.

'A-ha!' shouted the Yugoslav, 'you sly, sneaking English with your "on the one hand, on the other hand". Small wonder no one trusts you or knows which side of the struggle you are really on.'

And the Russian, when he could get a word in, appeared to be reciting a speech by someone else, which seemed to be a furious lecture on the evils of two-faced objectivism. He managed at the same time to include an attack upon the Yugoslav who was apparently so poorly disciplined that he permitted himself to be provoked and lose his temper in the presence of two westerners—one of whom, by the way, had a camera and was no doubt going to take advantage of feeble Yugoslav security measures to photograph important military installations.

Naturally, we all separated in dudgeon so soon as the transport situation permitted, but not before irreparable harm had been done to all the international relations involved. I escaped to look at the palace of the late King Nicholas of Montenegro, which was known as The Billiards on account of what happened years before when Nicholas, too, thought a little tourism and personal contacting would do him a power of good. In pursuit of this aim he went to England to see King Edward VII and the thing that impressed him was the prevalence of billiards in Britain.

He bought a couple of full-size billiards tables, and landed them on the shore at Kotor, and teams of peasants—there was no proper road then—had to run with them on their backs up a precipitous mountain path and right across the plateau to Cettinje to deliver them at the Palace.

The incident caused ill-will among the peasantry and fanned the spirit of unrest in the country, and Nicholas spent so much time playing billiards he did not have enough left to attend to domestic and international politics, and came to grief. Just one more proof of the dangers of gadding about and getting to know foreigners.

CLAUD COCKBURN

The Chairman, in his Report, Said . . .

Written after reading the headline PLEA FOR BRIGHTNESS
IN ANNUAL REPORT *in 'The Times'*

BEFORE putting before you the gross trading profits of the company for the year 1956, folks, I am sure you would wish me to say a few words about an incident of a humorous nature which befell your Chairman as I was wending my way hither. The incident is fully described in the copy of this Report which has been circulated with the accounts, so that I do not propose to burden you again at this time with the details of the affair, but only to add that this makes the fifth comical contretemps in which one or other of your directors has been involved during the past financial year—an improvement of over 40 per cent on the figures for 1955. Laughter, properly directed and controlled, is a valuable asset, and it will be the constant concern of the Board in the future, as in the past, to promote it by every means within their power.

Turning to the combined profit and loss account, the gross trading profit of £2,617,206 represents an increase of £50,542 over the previous year's working, and I am sure you will agree with the Board's view that this, in the prevailing conditions, is whizzo. Production of hot re-rolled slag has been well maintained and the slight falling-off of stripped sheets (a phrase to which your Chairman has devoted considerable care) is of a seasonal nature and not calculated to spoil your directors' sleep. Pig-iron, you may be amused to hear, dropped with a clang—to 3,886 tons, a new low record in the history of your rollicking Company.

I have some further figures here about liquid assets, provision for depreciation, and the writing-down of capital, which I would read to you if there was the faintest likelihood of your understanding a single word of it. All this jiggery-pokery is in any case included in the printed copy of the Report, together with my customary complaints about crippling taxation which I have this year presented in a jocular style that will, I hope, commend itself to shareholders. I propose therefore, with your permission, to take as read about fourteen paragraphs of balance sheetery and re-rolled platitudes and proceed at once to the only item in which our shareholders—whose presence, may I say, at our Annual General Meetings, even in such limited numbers, is a source of genuine amazement to the Board—take the slightest interest. We recommend, in short, a final dividend of 18 per cent on the Ordinary Stock, which with the interim dividend of 15 per cent already declared makes, as nearly as I can work it out in my present carefree mood, a total of 33 per cent. What do you think of that, boys and girls?

The Board feels, and I am sure that shareholders in their dumb way will agree, that this is a result which reflects the greatest credit on our General Manager and the loyal and efficient service of the whole staff. All the same, I don't know what the devil I am thinking about, thanking the staff in this way out of their proper turn. Gratitude to the staff comes at the end, as you will see if you turn to your

printed copies of the Report. I have first to tell you how sorry you will be to hear that Mr O. P. Cromer, who has served your Board unsparingly for seventy-five years, has at last decided to retire. It is not easy to be bright at such a moment, but I know Mr Cromer will not mind my saying in his presence—for he is as deaf as a post, and will continue to wag his head and make deprecatory gestures whatever I may say—I know he will forgive me for saying that if ever a man deserves to retire, he does. He carries with him into retirement the good wishes of the Company and a pension of £1,250, which will be a charge on the Consolidated Fund—though not, I am sure you will agree with me in thinking, for long.

I have also to record, with genuine regret, the loss of our Overseas Manager, whose broad humanity, ripe judgment and profound knowledge of pig-iron and cold smelting processes, particularly in the field of pressed bolts and tubings, will be greatly missed. He had a genius for friendship, which made him an ideal man to send overseas.

Turning, in accordance with the agreed policy of your Board, to brighter things, I am sure you would wish me, on your behalf, to thank the whole staff, which I have already done. It only remains, therefore, for me to say that their efforts have contributed in no small measure to the satisfactory account of our undertakings which I have been able to lay before you. Or, to put it another way, if none of them had done any of the work they are paid for, we should have sacked the lot—and well they know it. These considerations encourage me to hope that next year, provided nothing happens to reduce our profits, I shall be in a position to entertain you with an even brighter and breezier review.

The Report and Accounts were adopted amid scenes of unparalleled gaiety.

H. F. ELLIS

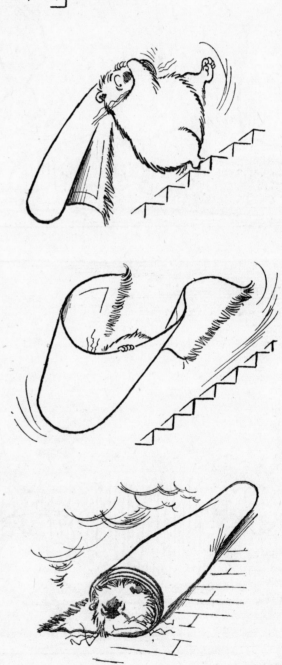

Off the Beat

For Nevil Shute, from a fellow ex-Serviceman

SHE was a good big hefty wench, with a nice friendly grin and no fal-lals about her at all. I liked the way her nose shone. It was the sort of nose you could sit across a desk from, day in, day out, without its taking your mind off the job in hand. I knew she would make a good secretary right away, which of course was what I needed, for a fellow without hands can't very well work a typewriter; and, besides, dictating helps me to get the words down more or less as they come to me, which I find helps the readability along. I do not set up to be a fancy stylist, as I've said elsewhere; but merely do my best to actually tell a story, as opposed to writing one. This may be why they call me a Prince of Storytellers; though naturally the 'Prince' part is so much rot.

I cannot deny, however, that the latest Australian *opus, A Place Called Tararaboomdiay*, wasn't getting on as fast as it should. Poor Sal did her utmost; she filled my favourite pipe, stuck it between my teeth, and lit it for me, but still the stuff, that day, just refused to flow.

'What do you think's lacking, Sal?' I asked her finally. 'The patriotic note? No, the Queen's Dominion Visit takes care of that. Misfortune stoically borne? Well, what about when the rabbits overrun the farm, and the gallant kangaroo . . .'

She said 'Want me to tell you? Honest Injun? You've left out the war.'

'But young Tim goes for a Burton over Berlin.'

'That's only an incident. Oh Norman, don't you see? All your big successes, beginning with *Flat Spin*, were books about the war *itself*. That's why they sold, and go on selling. Because for most members of the British public, those days really *were* their finest hour. The black-out, the raids, the queues, the shelters, helped bring people—total strangers—together in a sort of, oh I don't know, camaraderie, and it's that spirit they can only recapture by reading about it. Why, you yourself had your uniform edition bound in khaki. Mean to tell me you never wish the dear old sirens could wail again? Or wake up and hear Jerry overhead?'

She stopped abruptly, her cheeks flushing red. It was the longest speech I had ever heard her make, and I could see she was panting with sincerity.

I said quietly 'Too true, Sal. But look'—I nodded towards the shelf that housed my books—'I've been through nearly every branch of the Services already —*Wizard Prang, Up the Spout, Hush-Hush, The Deep End* . . .'

She grinned suddenly. 'I know one you haven't. C.M.P.S. Don't worry. I haven't forgotten the D.B. effort, *A Prison Make*, about the Glasshouse padre who was a kind of saint. No, I was thinking of the Distaff jobs.'

I said, after a pause, 'Is that what you were in? The Women's Provost Corps, or whatever they call them now?'

'Me? No. I was an A.T.S. P.T. Sergeant. You know. In the gym. But I had a buddy——' she paused, and her nose shone with seriousness. 'It's a long yarn,' she warned me. 'You see, Norman, to me this girl was— well, a sort of heroine.'

'Maybe the very thing I'm looking for,' I said. 'Attagirl—I'm all ears.'

Senior Sergeant Jane Pebble, R.W.M.P.—or whatever the corps is called (I didn't make a note of it at the time)—was the daughter of a porter at some college in Oxford, who had worn himself to a shadow in order to send her to a posh girls' school where they even taught Deportment. Not that Janey was ever

'Would you care to say grace?'

much good at that sort of tripe. She was better at hockey; it was stopping the ball with her nose when she was playing in goal that made them take the cartilage out and caused the other girls to call her 'Butch'. There wasn't much of the shadow about Janey, whatever her Pa may have been like. She was a strapping, brawny piece even as a kid, about twice Sal's size; the kind of girl that carries a good, honest smell of dog and horse about with her, and that every decent clean-living Britisher really loves in his heart. When the Hitler war broke out, naturally she was ra'ring to do her bit; especially as Pa had dug out his 1918 Sergeant-major's Service-dress, joined the L.D.V., and started cleaning the musket his O.C. had issued

him with. One day, while he was doing this, an old charge dating from Balaclava, that was hidden up inside, went off and blew his head away; but by that time Janey, who had joined the A.T.S., was too busy training to be a Regimental Policewoman to feel like blubbing for more than a few seconds when the news came through; but, of course, she was too brave to shed any tears in the end. Soon she was doing guard-duty at a big depot—that was where Sal first met her —with her red armband on (I think), and putting the fear of A.F.B. 252 (if this is what they call a charge-sheet in her mob) into any A.T. improperly dressed: even by so much as an undone bootlace.

Janey was no respecter of anyone; she would not

think twice about chewing up any male personnel she saw doing anything prejudicial to G.O. and M.D., and once, when a gunner private suggested what she could do to herself, she gave him such a biff on the earhole that his side-cap flew off right under a bus. Of course it was not long before she had a pair of white-blancoed tapes sewn on either sleeve, and got posted to M.P. Headquarters in London where—I believe—the girls attached wore service caps with red tops and were allowed to put paint and powder on their faces; though Janey scorned to do anything so cissy. Sal lost sight of her in the meantime for a bit; and when they did manage to get together on their seven days, Jane had already picked up with this chap she called Frenchy. They'd met one night in the black-out, when Frenchy had perhaps had a few drinks and a bunch of spivs had set on him seven to one. Janey, of course, hearing the sound of a scrap, piled in right away; and between them they soon had the spivs beating an inglorious retreat. Not that Frenchy could not have managed it on his own; for he was apparently very strong, and when he and Janey wrestled together—in a friendly way on their day-passes, it took him only about fifteen minutes to have her securely pinned. Janey told Sal he was the only man she'd ever respected; because, being such a brawny girl, no other male had been able to master her in unarmed combat. Frenchy, it stands to reason, was not really a Frenchman—Janey wouldn't have touched anything like that, however Free he might have been; it was just a nickname she had for him: Sal couldn't remember, or never knew, why. She never saw Frenchy herself; it seemed he had some terribly Top Secret job to do with H.E.: in fact he was really a kind of top-rating civilian expert, though they'd put him into Army uniform—a major's, Sal thought Janey said.

He was always being posted or disappearing on these hush-hush parties; and Janey worried terribly until she saw him safely back, although she'd too much grit not to keep a stiff upper lip about it. It was during one of these absences that poor Janey dropped a clanger. She was made up Senior Sergeant by then, and was on her beat or patrol one night when a fearful row broke out in the black-out ahead; and what was plainly a deserter, pursued by shouting male C.M.P.s, headed straight for her, and what's more he was flourishing a pistol. She could see him plain, because some fool had left a blind half-up in one of the houses, and light fairly streamed across the pavement. Janey didn't hesitate. She hurled herself straight for his knees in a clean rugger tackle, and down they both went, the fellow catching his head a fearful crack on the kerb. Janey wasn't hurt, but the bloke lay still; and then suddenly, where she'd expected at least a pat on the back, a crowd of people—including the C.M.P.s—came rushing up and started to bawl her out like nobody's business. As she realized, through her bewilderment, much later, they were making some sort of documentary-propaganda film and this was a realistic outdoor chase-sequence, or something. Anyway, the supposed deserter was dashed away in an ambulance, and next day poor, dazed Janey came up before her O.C. It seems the chap was badly concussed and might die, and it looked as if Janey'd get broken down to private at the very least—if she wasn't had up for manslaughter.

This went on for days, right in the middle of the Normandy landings too; and buzz-bombs started coming over, to make things worse. Janey was frightfully rattled about Frenchy as well; she thought he'd be out there in the thick of it—and then, lo and behold, one night he walked right into the pub where they usually met, and in civvies. Janey couldn't believe her eyes. He wasn't his usual self either; he had let his hair grow long—a thing she never could abide,

even in a woman—and when a fly-bomb cut out at least a mile away he closed his eyes before the bang. But it was principally the way he talked, Sal said. He'd let his job get him down, and been to the trick-cyclist, who had sent him on ten days' sick and talked about a psychiatric discharge and Category 'E'. Worse still, he had begun to mumble about wanting to do something artistic when he got back in civvy-street; and at that Janey fairly let him have it. She said, in effect, that she was blowed if she'd have any pip-squeak scribblers or daubers shirking about when there was man's work to be done—she had pretty wide command of strong Service language—and the upshot was that Frenchy walked out on her there and then. Of course Janey was ready to make things up next day; she'd a quick temper, but it was soon over, and after all she loved Frenchy deeply, but he had vanished as if a v.1 had got him, and was nowhere to be found. Added to which, Janey came up before the c.o. this time; the film-chap was now safely on the mend, but the c.o. said there was nothing for it—they would have to get rid of her on medical grounds. Janey was stunned. She had never, even in her worst nightmares, envisaged having to leave the Service altogether. She almost broke down. Then, remembering in time that she was a Sergeant-major's daughter, she drew herself up, saluted—she wasn't on any actual charge—and left H.Q. in an absolute daze. It was then that the v.1 struck; she was in such misery that she had not even heard it cut out. Blast threw her to the ground; but she was up in a second and racing towards the crumbling house on the corner of the street. . . .

'She managed to hold up the roof with one hand until they got everyone out,' Sal told me, sitting dry-eyed but choky on the other side of the desk. 'Then it fell in on her. Somehow I don't think she wanted to hold it up any longer. . . . They let me see her in hospital before the end. She knew me all right. She put up one hand to the sergeant's stripes on her sleeve—she was still wearing her B.D. of course—and she managed to give a sort of grin. She said: "You see, Sal? They weren't able to strip me after all." And that was the end.'

There was a long silence. I felt a bit strangled myself. Then I said 'And Frenchy?'

'Oh, I heard later he'd gone back to his job. But somehow one of the bombs he fiddled with went bang and blew him all to glory, poor blighter.'

I grinned, 'Not quite *all*.' I held up my hooks. 'Just these.'

She stared at me in wonder. She said, hardly above a whisper, 'Oh, *Norman . . . Darling . . .* But how could I have known?'

I said, '*Norman French*, you see—hence "Frenchy". It was Butch's great joke.' Then I said. 'Don't blub, darling. It's just one of these coincidences that don't happen much in real life—though people swallow them whole in my books.'

The tears dried instantly on Sal's round cheeks. She said, 'You mean—you're going to make a novel of this? After all?'

'Why not?' I said. 'We'll build a memorial to Butch, together. And I know just the title for it—*In the Nick*. She was taken just in the nick of time, you see—to save her sergeant's stripes. And that ties up with her being a woman M.P., too. What do you say, Sal?'

Sal grinned. She picked up her shorthand pad and poised her pencil over it. 'I say: let's go—Your Royal Highness!'

J. MACLAREN-ROSS

Cartwright and the Need for Sleep

MY HUSBAND Cartwright would describe himself as a realist, but he is not above harbouring certain illusions. One of these used to be that he did not snore: or if he did, it was in such a manner no reasonable person could be disturbed by him. In any case there was a cure. He snored only when lying on his back, and, at a request to turn over, would turn over and peace would be restored. There was a time when this was true.

Once, during the war, he had to share a tent on a desert survey with a man called Donaldson. Before they left Cairo I said to Donaldson: 'I'm afraid Cartwright snores slightly. He only does it when he's tired, of course, and only when lying on his back. If you say to him "Turn over, darling", he'll turn over and be quiet.'

'Must it be "Turn over, *darling*"?'

'Nothing else is effective.'

The next night Donaldson was wakened by Cartwright's snores. Sitting up in bed he commanded: 'Turn over.'

Cartwright remained flat on his back.

'Turn over, Cartwright.'

No move.

Then, reluctantly, in the fiercest tones, Donaldson said: 'Turn over, darling,' and with the slow, inevitable movement of a wave, Cartwright turned over and slept in silence.

The time came when this formula ceased to be effective. When Cartwright turned there would be a short peace, then the noise would start again. When I could endure it no longer I would wake him up.

'Darling, wake up. You're making a frightful noise.'

'Me? Impossible. I was lying on my side.'

'That makes no difference nowadays.'

'But any doctor will tell you that people can't snore on their sides.'

'Well, I should know better. I've been awake since midnight.'

'The trouble is, darling, you're becoming neurotic. I wasn't even asleep. I was just lying thinking. I had my eyes open.'

'Then you not only snore on your back and on your side, you snore with your eyes open.'

'You're being ridiculous. And *please* don't wake me up again.'

One day he discussed the matter with a scientific friend who said he had done research on the problem of snoring. People, he said, snored when lying on their backs because the tongue fell against the soft palate, causing it to vibrate. He lay on the floor to demonstrate his theory. Cartwright insisted on my watching the performance. The scientific friend, flat on his back, snored furiously, then rolled over on his side and ceased to snore. His tongue, he said, had fallen into its natural position, so snoring became impossible.

'Now are you convinced?' Cartwright asked me.

'Of course I'm not.'

'Darling, you're being unreasonable.'

Like many people addicted to theory he was badly betrayed by experience. He did not, needless to say, lend himself willingly to experience. The occasion was forced upon him. It happened last year when he was invited by a student body to lecture on Scottish Drama at the Edinburgh Festival. He travelled north with his three fellow lecturers. They arrived to find that owing to Festival overcrowding it had been possible to book only two rooms for the four of them. Each room, however, contained two beds, so no great hardship was imposed on the lecturers. Cartwright was to share with a very large, good-natured man called Peabody, and was pleased rather than not by the prospect. So sociable is his nature that he finds it a strain to suffer even a night in solitude. His only fear was that Peabody would object to his reading in bed. I sometimes objected—usually when, having been too busy to absorb them during the day, he rattled his way through a collection of newspapers.

'I read in bed a bit,' said Cartwright; 'hope it won't disturb you.'

'Nothing disturbs me.'

'That's splendid. My wife's rather a light sleeper.'

'I sleep like the dead,' said Peabody. 'I'm off as soon as I put my head on the pillow and I don't wake up till morning.'

Another theory held by Cartwright is that human beings need very little sleep. Sleep, he believes, is a superstition of mine. He needs no more than four or five hours. Night was the time when he 'caught up with his reading'.

Cartwright is a busy man made more busy by the fact that he gives so much time to his friends. Before

leaving for Edinburgh he had been too busy to make notes for his lectures. He might have made them on the train, but with three companions willing to listen to him all the way, work would have been a waste of opportunity. He intended settling down to it on arrival, but the others were in jovial mood, inclined towards an evening of good food and drink, and Cartwright was easily persuaded to join them. They were all wine drinkers, but they felt they owed it to Scotland to drink what they kept calling 'the wine of the country'. They had an evening on whisky, which is generously served in Edinburgh. By the time they reached their rooms Peabody was so drowsy he had to be assisted to bed. He was asleep even before his head touched the pillow.

Cartwright, drowsy or not, had now to apply himself to his lecture notes. He sat up in bed surrounded by books on the Scottish Drama which he had supposed, before this time, to be non-existent. Although he is not a silent man, he likes quiet when he works. He had just uncapped his fountain-pen when Peabody gave a first snore. It was slight and brief. Cartwright ignored it. That, he supposed, was the sort of noise he occasionally made himself. It need disturb no one. The first snore, however, was followed by a much louder one. Then, as though, after a trial attempt, an engine had got under way, there was a crescendo of snores that ended in a spluttering roar like the bursting of a water-tank. This climax achieved, Peabody set out to achieve it again.

I might find such a noise disturbing, but Cartwright decided he did not. He fixed his eyes on his text-book. He was concentrating. Peabody repeated the water-tank theme a dozen times before Cartwright realized he was unable to understand a word he read. He looked appealingly at Peabody, then remembered that people snored only when on their backs. Peabody was flat on his back. He must be turned upon his side.

Cartwright ordered him: 'Turn over, Peabody.'

Peabody did not move.

'Turn over, darling.'

This famous formula had no effect on Peabody. He was an unmarried man. Cartwright decided to move him by force. He rose and started tugging and pushing at Peabody. Cartwright is a big man, but Peabody was much bigger. He was a dead weight. At last Peabody was moved on to his side, but as soon as he was left unsupported he slid round again on to his back. This happened half a dozen times.

There was only one pillow on each bed. Cartwright realized he must sacrifice his as a prop for Peabody. When he wedged it in, Peabody's vast body remained on its side.

Cartwright returned to bed to work. He had read half a dozen lines when Peabody spluttered slightly,

HOW TO INCREASE YOUR HEIGHT

Sprod

then gave a preliminary snore. Cartwright could not believe his ears. Peabody snored again, then settled to a new theme, a rhythmic trumpeting on a deep note. Cartwright gazed at him. It was true—Peabody was lying on his side and snoring. After some moments he decided the trouble was he had put Peabody on the wrong side.

He rose again, then, tugging and pushing, rolled Peabody on to the other side and wedged the pillow back again. Now he would have peace in which to work.

Peabody, perhaps disturbed by the experience, remained silent slightly longer than before. Cartwright was just congratulating himself on having achieved quiet when Peabody snored. Not possible. Cartwright's heart sank. He paused in apprehension. Soon Peabody's snores were rising again to full blast. It was as though a procession of elephants, emerging from jungle into sunlight, trumpeted in turn. It was a monotonous procession bringing not even the relief of an exploding water-tank.

Cartwright had to admit that people did snore on their sides. This extension of knowledge brought no comfort. Still, it was not Peabody's fault. Anyone might snore. The reasonable listener did not permit himself to be disturbed by such a trifle. Cartwright kept his eyes on his book and again told himself he

was concentrating on his work. But he was not. When he was not listening to Peabody he was fabricating excuses for Peabody or telling himself that he had, after all, chosen to work at night. Anyone else would be asleep. At the thought of sleep he realized how tired he was. He had travelled that day from London to Edinburgh. He had dined well and drunk deeply. He had a heavy day's talking behind him. He realized that human beings did, after all, need some sleep. He needed it now.

He decided to leave Scottish Drama until the morning. He turned off the light and settled down to sleep. But he could not sleep. The snores vibrated through his head. As sleep overcame him a roar would buffet him back to wakefulness. He was in the midst of telling himself he could not blame Peabody —when the benignity of his nature suddenly collapsed beneath him. He fell into fury. He sat up and put on the light. He shouted: 'Peabody, for heaven's sake, shut up!'

The shout seemed to stun Peabody. He was silent for a full minute, then, grunting and spluttering, he recovered himself. He struggled round as though against fearful odds, then, lying spread-eagled on Cartwright's pillow, he started out again upon the water-tank theme.

Cartwright, seldom made angry, can, on rare occasions, touch upon frenzy. He touched upon it now. He picked up one of his shoes and bounced it upon Peabody's belly, shouting: 'Shut up! Shut up! Shut up!' The shoe caused no more than a moment's hiatus in sound. The second shoe did not even do that.

Cartwright opened his book again. He read one paragraph half a dozen times. He could make nothing of it. Somewhere a clock struck three. He had made one lecture note: 'Where's your Wullie Shakespeare now?' What the answer was he neither knew nor cared. He wanted only to sleep.

At four o'clock he decided he could bear the water-tank theme no longer. He rose and crossed to the other bed. Standing there he snarled: 'Peabody, I hate you!' Then he set about turning Peabody back on to his side. When he again held his pillow on his hand he was filled with a wild, exultant desire to smother Peabody's snores beneath it. Overcoming this, he wedged it behind the body again and stood and listened until Peabody was well back into the elephant theme. He said: 'Peabody, I could murder you.'

Back in bed, Cartwright began to shiver with weariness and frustration. He put out the light and tried again to sleep. He covered his ears with his

ROY DAVIS

hands. They did no more than take the edge off the noise. After an hour or two he shouted: 'For goodness' sake, Peabody, shut up!'

At intervals, to relieve his almost unendurable exasperation, he bawled out: 'Wake up, Peabody, or I shall wring your neck,' or '. . . fling you out of bed', or '. . . brain you with the electric fire'.

Peabody slept, sublimely unaware of these dangers.

Some time after dawn exhaustion overcame Cartwright's senses so that the snoring came to him as no more than an attendant of dreams. Sometimes it seemed the rhythm of the 'Flying Scotsman', sometimes the engine of a ship, sometimes the ruthless hammer-blows of a man driven to exterminate his tormentor.

A cheerful Scottish voice broke in on all this to say: 'Come along, now, sir. You wanted to be wakened at eight o'clock sharp.'

Cartwright struggled up in bed and took his breakfast tray on his knee. He was due in the lecture room at nine-thirty. He might, if he ate and dressed hurriedly, have half an hour to give to Scottish Drama.

He was in a stupor. The wardrobe looking-glass showed him his face, drawn, ghastly, moist-looking, the eyes rimmed with red and oozing tears. He could not keep from yawning. He looked at his breakfast with disgust.

Sitting up in the other bed, Peabody was aglow with health and eating with appetite. He met Cartwright's glance with a coy smile.

Cartwright, who had had it in mind to make some wryly humorous reference to his disturbed night, now decided to say nothing. What was past, was past. He simply said 'Hope you slept well?'

Peabody's coy smile grew more coy. 'I hardly like to mention it,' he said, 'but—you know what, Cartwright? You talk in your sleep.'

OLIVIA MANNING

Half an Hour in China

Mr Hu had seemed a little reserved when I first telephoned the Embassy. I quite understood. Relatively new to London diplomatic life, Chairman Mao Tse-tung's representatives naturally lean towards a touch of native inscrutability when breezy strangers ring up with a demand to be shown over a Chinese typewriter. I think Mr Hu's first impulse, as a matter of fact, was to deny the existence of any such thing, but his better nature, or his concern for Communism's cultural prestige, got the better of him. He finally admitted that there was a Chinese typewriter. As to my seeing it, he would have to inquire, and let me know.

A week passed. No doubt the line to Peking was busy. I was abandoning the typewriter, and planning instead to write about China's obstructionist attitude to Western journalists, when the summons unexpectedly came. Soon Mr Hu was welcoming me over the threshold of the People's Republic with an immensely cordial grip of his small, cold hand, and leading the way to a sitting-room of spacious comfort not the least overdone. There was nothing to show that I was in China; nothing Chinese at all, except Mr Hu and the cigarette he gave me. No portrait of the Chairman. It was warm. I said so, removing my coat. 'But not, I trust, stuffy?' said Mr Hu, springing up in some anxiety, prepared to smash a window if my comfort required it. His English was fluent, but often favoured an upward, interrogative cadence, so that I was not always certain whether he was being agreeable or sceptical. We opened with the weather. I said that in England a cold morning sometimes became a warm afternoon. 'Yes?' said Mr Hu.

'I read the other day,' I told him, conscious that my pause had been too short, but anxious to place the visit on a rational footing, 'that your newspapers are now to be printed left to right, instead of top to bottom.'

'Yes?'

'And I somehow got to wondering about Chinese typewriters. I thought I'd like to see one.'

He asked if I spoke Chinese, and I said 'No'. I may even have said 'No?' It seemed a good time to learn. After all, as I understood the language it was quite simple. Just a lot of pictures. A child could read it. In fact the only thing that I found really puzzling about Chinese was its system of dealing with proper names. It's obviously easy enough to draw a picture meaning a house or a tree or a mountain, but to draw one meaning John Foster Dulles or Llandudno is another matter. I put this to Mr Hu, and he said that that too was simple. You just wrote down the pictures of the sounds in the name. He obligingly demonstrated on my own, and it came out at five pictures, swift, intricate and neat, with what looked like an expensive American fountain pen. I asked what it meant. 'Nothing,' he said. There was no context. A character's meaning is governed by the characters around it. I pressed him, so he studied my Chinese name again to oblige me, and found in it Cloth, True, Low, Virtue and Ism. 'Ism?' I said. Mr Hu gestured. 'Capitalism? Communism?' He gave me an affable little nudge, and chuckled. 'Toryism?'

But a proper gravity returned as he described the plan for simplifying the language, a plan of which the horizontal printing of newspapers is only a beginning. Apparently it can do with simplifying, after all. There are characters involving as many as twenty-three separate strokes of brush or pen. These will be reduced to as few as three. There are more than a thousand different characters all meaning the same thing and having the same sound. They will go. The innumerable dialects will be reduced to one. It struck me that there would be room for other improvements. For instance, most of the 'pictures' aren't pictures at all: they may be merely devices to represent abstract ideas, to express nothing more than the spoken sound of the idea to be conveyed. Many characters look different and have different mean-

ings, but are phonetically indistinguishable; there are, for instance, several dozen words pronounced *shih*, but with meanings as delightfully varied as Lion, Beginning, Poetry, House and Corpse. Absolute lucidity is hard to be sure of, and a hasty translation of Confucius's 'Oppressive government is fiercer than a tiger' could easily end up instead with something about nagging wives or the high cost of fish, leaving the Confucian worse confounded. Again, many of the characters look pretty much alike even when they aren't: the standard dictionary of the Emperor K'ang Hsi listed about forty-nine thousand of them, so similarities were bound to creep in; moreover, there must have been additions lately, to fill the need for such modern expressions as Agricultural Producers' Co-operatives, or Imperialist Bureaucrat-Capitalist. In fact, as I said to Mr Hu, it was a wonder that after five thousand years of this some pruning and revision hadn't been done before. (I was glad that I said this, because it gave him an opportunity to whip in his commercial: 'The political and economic unity of China demands the adoption of a

95

universal national language.') The language has virtually no grammar, which must be a boon to Chinese schoolchildren; but it also has absolutely no alphabet, which must be a headache for Chinese typists.

Brought full circle in this way Mr Hu led me out into the hall. The typewriter stood on a table, decently draped with a white cloth. Ordinarily its place was on the Embassy's fifth floor, but that was a long way for me to have to go, he explained. Here was characteristic courtesy—though in fact I shouldn't at all have minded trailing up there, all among the secret documents and military appreciations.

Mr Hu stepped forward and removed the cloth. 'Chinese typewriter?' he announced.

In a way, it was a bit of an anti-climax. I had expected something between a hand-loom and a linen-press, but the thing was obviously of the genus typewriter by the platen, familiarly black and smooth and cylindrical, though fatter than those of the West. There was no keyboard. Instead, in the base of the machine, a packed tray of tiny square rubber stamps —about five thousand characters. Over them hung a beaked arm, movable in all directions, unresisting, like the steering-wheel in a car with the front jacked up. 'But how?' I said. 'Simple to work,' said Mr Hu. He took the arm and hovered like a cormorant over the rich shoal beneath, then banged it down. The beak snatched up a fish; smacked it on the paper, threw it back in its place. 'Quite simple?' said Mr Hu. I peered at the printed impression and asked what it said. 'Nothing,' said Mr Hu. Of course, no context.

With permission, I typed a word or two. It might have meant anything. Or nothing. After that the occasion seemed virtually over. Two points struck me. One was that Chinese typists won't be greatly worried by the new horizontalization policy—it's simply a matter of feeding the paper in sideways; the other, that tracking down the right word out of those five thousand, all tiny, similar and backwards, must make life in a Chinese typing pool a long series of pregnant silences. I put this to Mr Hu. He shrugged it aside. Naturally, he said, they had to learn where they all were. Moreover, there were several other trays, interchangeable according to the nature of the document under transcription . . .

As I stepped back on to British soil he asked me to let him have a copy of the article. He said it might make his typist laugh. I hope it will. I can't think of a more deserving case.

J. B. BOOTHROYD

The Delegation

WE CROWDED from the anteroom
  To meet him face to face.
We sidled ceremoniously
  Each man into his place,
Hoping our numbers might off-set
  A certain lack of case.

We sat and faced the Minister,
  Packed almost cheek to cheek.
Against us on his either hand,
  Inscrutable and sleek,
Sat six homunculi who spoke
  When he was slow to speak.

In words that were the work of days
  We argued and appealed
On several arguable points
  And all that wider field
Of what we knew he knew would come
  And did not mean to yield.

He showed a tolerance of mind
  Much more than merely just.
He seemed to share our point of view
  On all that we discussed.
His calculated sympathy
  Rebuked our deep mistrust.

His eyes were luminous and large
  And innocent of guile;
His hands were smooth and white and
    square
  And gestured all the while;
And all his words were softly turned
  And spoken with a smile:

He picked them with a loving care
  That made them seem profound.
They dropped directly to the point
  And yet went round and round,
And seemed to weave a complex web
  Of non-committal sound.

He talked. We talked. He talked again,
  And neither quite believed
The other won, but parted so
  And, parting, each received
A sense of duty done if not
  Of very much achieved.

B. B.-P. DURHAM

Come into the Beuk

WE PAY 11·462*d* in the £ for the Public Library, I and the other burghers; 7·732*d* less than for the Police and 10·802*d* more than for the Civil Defence. On June 8 this year we had 67,462 books out among the lot of us, including three that had got among the tennis-rackets we keep behind our piano, on which a fine of 1*s* 7*d* was owing. Twenty-five per cent of my fellow burghers are what the Librarian calls 'active readers', by which he seems to mean readers who don't just wander into the library for a sit down or to get away from their relations, but actually come along and lug a proportion of the books home with them. Some of these active readers are known to read some of the books they borrow. Sixty per cent of the active reading burghers are at work on the non-fiction section, and the rest are assisting at the protracted funeral of the Novel (see *The Listener*, Jan., Feb., March, April, May, etc.) with 25,984·2 corpses cluttering up their houses on the night of June 8, including one in our airing-cupboard on which we had to pay 3*s* 4*d*.

Most of these statistics were provided by the Librarian, a shrewdly distrustful, involuntarily communicative man with everything cut and withered at his finger-tips, and a tendency to talk about things like 'the position with regard to the borrowing situation at a given moment'. He was not happy about my credentials.

'From the press?' he inquired, running his eye over my three-quarter-length cape, anti-gas.

'Not exactly *from*,' I said.

'I can give you some figures,' he said.

I wanted to ask if he thought librarians began to look like books at a certain stage, the way fishmongers

resembled fish; and whether they came to hate readers as bus-conductors hate passengers. What percentage of librarians were active reading burghers in private life, with or without pianos and/or airing-cupboards?

'With regard to fiction for, um, purchase,' he was saying, 'that is in the hands of experienced senior library personnel specially trained in selection, largely based, of course, on the best critical and authoritative opinion with regard to current trends.'

His nose was as sharp as a pen and I felt like W. Pickles earning every penny he screws out of the B.B.C. Was he courting, or had he read any embarrassing books lately?

'Very interesting,' I assured him. 'Significant.'

When he had given me some more figures he rose to his feet, shoes black, size 10, narrow fitting. 'The proper course, of course, where it is wished to make inquiries is to make application to the Chief Librarian. As a matter of courtesy. The Chief Librarian does not, of course, himself grant interviews.'

'Of course not.'

'But instructions would normally be given to an appropriate junior official, depending on the nature of the inquiries which were to be made and of which the Chief Librarian would normally require a record to be filed. For reference purposes. Details of the nature of the specific inquiries should be stated in the letter of application which would be addressed to the Chief Librarian. Permission would almost certainly be granted, but the letter should be sent.'

I had my hand on the door with the words ONLY STAFF on the frosted glass. There was a girl at a table working on a display notice:

BOOKS FOR THE HANDYMA——

'Well, I—um,' I said.

'As a matter of courtesy,' the Librarian said, and I was outside, facing the fiction shelves U—Z, among a crowd of active reading burghers, peering and weaving, twitching and grieving like Dylan's hens, along the rows of books.

As things stand, you can borrow three non-fiction books and one fiction; but *avant-garde* assistant librarians are already talking of a massive reorganization of the system which will have the effect of reversing the ratio, bringing it back into line with the latest

ROY DAVIS

neo-Victorian sociological *What-would-you-like*? *Well-you-can't-have-it* trends.

This is no place for an exhaustive analysis of the operation of the best critical and public-authoritative taste in fiction, but reading mostly along the upper shelves on account of a touch of lumbago you find most of the authors you would expect for $11 \cdot 462d$ in the £—with one or two notable gaps, probably caused by reading burghers becoming exceptionally active in an effort to out-do the June 8 figures. Some novels bear the figure 8 in gilt upon their spines, and this means they can be taken out on a non-fiction ticket. I asked the Librarian about this.

'This figure 8——'

'Yes?'

'Who, um——?'

'The decision is taken by senior personnel in conjunction with the best critical and authoritative critical authorities, with a view to——'

'Getting the burghers to read proper books, and shifting some of the heavy stuff that clogs the—um——?'

'With a view to indicating that the work or works in question are felt to reach the highest levels of, um, literature.'

'How long must an author be dead in order to——?'

'There is no question of an author's being necessarily dead.'

Nor is there when you come to look at the shelves,

though it obviously helps. *Bagehot, Balzac, Bennett, Burney, Collins, W., Conrad, Defoe, De Morgan, Dickens, Dostoevsky, Dumas, Eliot, Fielding, Flaubert, France, Galsworthy, Gide*—16 to 1 on the dear departed, the one respectably not a novelist and the Frenchmen making the running.

One would have liked to press the point, to get at least a keyhole glimpse of senior personnel at their summit talks, bestowing and, on occasion, withdrawing the hallmark. Who gave it to G. K. Chesterton? And who took it away? Who boldly distinguished between Sitwells E., O. and S.? Who spoke for Kipling and who ditched Hugh Walpole? Why had Lord 'Jorkens-Has-a-Large-Whisky' Dunsany so brief an hour of glory? And can anything be done about Lord 'Last-Days-of-Pompeii' Lytton?

Vexed questions all, and unsuitable for mention in a letter to a senior official. Nor would one willingly asperse the hawk-like vigilance of appropriate personnel, though there are one or two eightless volumes we are watching pretty closely—*David Elginbrod*, for instance, by George MacDonald, LL.D., author of *Alec Forbes of Howglen, Sir Gibbie, Salted With Fire*, etc., and dedicated TO THE MEMORY OF LADY NOEL BYRON WITH A LOVE STRONGER THAN DEATH, pp. 412. Published in crown 8vo at 3s. 6d. and still in the original cloth gilt, this Hurst and Blackett novel remained steadfast on its shelf even in the frantic days of week ending June 11. It begins: 'Meg! Whaur are ye gaein' that get, like a wull shuttle? Come in to the beuk.' If it doesn't get an 8 pretty soon, some of us active reading burghers are going to buy its discharge and present it to the Chief Librarian.

WILLIAM THORNTON

Mum's the Word

ROYAL families are the first in any land to live their lives in public, for the sake of the People. But other, humbler families exist, capable of making a similar sacrifice. One such is a family named McCorquodale. The lives of two of its members, Mrs Barbara McCorquodale and Mrs Gerald Legge, have for long been open best-sellers.

Lately a benevolent bookseller gave a banquet in honour not only of these two ladies but of a third: the mother of one and the grandmother of the other, named Mrs Polly Cartland. To The McCorquodale Story and The Legge Show, already familiar to millions, is thus now added The Cartland Story.

The impresario of the trilogy is Mrs McC. (Barbara C.), who has written a book called *Polly: My Wonderful Mother*.

Polly, we read in its pages, herself had a Wonderful Mother, who not only enjoyed 'exquisite feet and ankles' but was 'not the sort of girl to be kissed under the stairs'. She had also a Wonderful Grandfather, 'exceedingly good-looking with fine chiselled features, bright blue eyes, fair curly hair and side-whiskers'; a Wonderful Great-Uncle, who invented the V.C.; a Wonderful Father, 'an outstandingly good dancer,' who climbed Mont Blanc; and a Wonderful Uncle, who was Champion Archer of England. Wonderful Polly had dancing brown eyes and an irresistible charm, moreover 'the gift of looking smart in a silk petticoat'. She was also a good fast bowler, and once took five wickets in a match.

Loved in turn by one of the most attractive men in the county (Worcs.), 'red-haired and devastatingly good-looking,' and by a Scotsman with 'that indefinable look of being a gentleman,' she finally married Bertie, 'six foot tall, good-looking, with light blue eyes which always seemed to have a twinkle in them, and exceedingly smart'—also with his own private hansom.

After a 'ripping year' or so of marriage, Barbara, the future Mrs McC., was born, with, as she (Mrs McC.) writes, 'very well-shaped legs, and feet,' destined moreover to be 'very pretty, being tall with fair hair, greenish eyes and a very clear pink-and-white complexion', and to enjoy 'an instantaneous success' at Bembridge. While her brother said 'I shall be Prime Minister', Barbara said 'I shall get to know everybody—everybody in London'.

She got to know Hugo, 'charming and an outstandingly good dancer'; Pingo, the son of a baronet; Peter, 'good-looking, very rich'; and, after refusing forty-five other proposals, she married a Mr McCorquodale, only son of an 'enormously wealthy father', then another Mr McCorquodale, 'quiet, charming and one of the finest game shots in England'. She also wrote fifty-eight best-sellers, from *A Virgin in Mayfair* to *Escape from Passion*, from *Again This Rapture* to *Love Me For Ever*, together with a quantity of letters to her Wonderful Mum: 'angelicest, rippingest . . . so utterly splendid . . . *marvellous.*'

Meanwhile, a Wonderful Daughter was born, a 'lovely child', christened Raine, much as her half-brother was later christened Glen and the heroine of *The Kiss of the Devil* Skye. At the age of one she was blessed by the Kiss of Princess Elizabeth and the

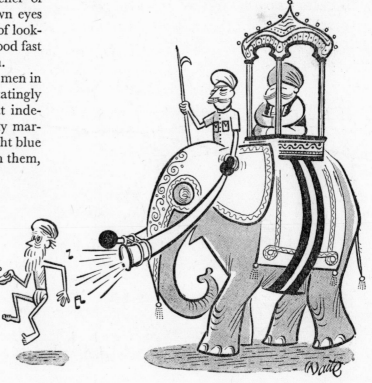

remark 'What a lovely fat baby!' Nine months later, 'with great aplomb and pose (*sic*),' she presented a bouquet to the Duchess of York. Later still, 'growing prettier every year,' she rose to be 'one of the most beautiful girls in England', with 'a sweet, gentle, friendly nature combined with a lot of real intelligence'. As such she became Débutante of the Year and was married to Mr Legge, 'extremely clever, charming and rich,' moreover the son of a Chief Constable and the heir to an Earl.

Lynette, the prize débutante of *Blue Heather*—'She was lovely, she had glamour, she had a figure which rivalled the measurements of any professional model, and she had a social background. What girl could ask for more?'—wanted only to marry a 'catch' and be 'front page news'. Raine, on the other hand, won a gold medal for oratory. 'A fearless and outspoken critic,' her Brains are for ever in Trust for the People in general and the City Council of Westminster in particular.

They know that she believes in Love ('Not only *sex* love, but love of children or a little kitten or humanity'); the Conservative Party (Sir Anthony Eden is not only 'one of the best-looking men in England to-day' but has 'perfect integrity and perfect manners, and these are the things that count most with a man'); British fashions (Mr Hartnell—'he does make you feel heavenly'—has done 'so much to improve our national taste' and so of course to raise our spiritual values); also showing the flag, preventing schoolchildren from singing dirty songs, and keeping the tea-cups clean at London Airport.

So now here they are in the flesh, this Wonderful Trio symbolic of all that is best in English county life, all three of them posed in a glare of lights before four hundred banqueters, fourteen photographers and a round half-dozen McCorquodales. Mrs McC. in blue (royal) with five rows of pearls, Mrs L. in red (tomato and salmon) with two, both poodle-curled and plumed like high-stepping thoroughbreds, face up to the public ordeal without flinching, having proved their mettle before. Mrs C. in black (discreet), with four rows of pearls and a choker, faces it for the first time with similar fortitude, being made of similar stuff.

Other Wonderful Mums sit flanking them—a portrait painter with his, a TV announcer with hers. A Wonderful Viscount ('terribly good-looking,' with a 'beautiful smile' which always got him 'all the votes he needed') has come 'all the way from Worcestershire' to introduce them ('a pretty example of heredity . . . scintillating femininity . . . sterling attributes'). Then in turn they rise to talk of themselves and each other.

Mrs McC. explains that she has written the book, 'a Cavalcade of the Century,' not only with her pen but with her heart: 'She lit in all of us a flame to do well . . . We die and are buried but the English people go on.' Mrs L.: 'As long as we have such wonderful grandmothers England will always set an example to the rest of the civilized world.' Mrs C.: 'I'm not wonderful, but I have a wonderful family.'

Toasts are drunk from empty glasses. The impressed but not so wonderful banqueters feel like crying 'Three cheers for the Red, Black and Blue!' But the toastmaster forestalls them, putting an authoritative end to the proceedings. With a sigh and a tear they turn away. Soon the Wonderful Mummery is but a memory.

LORD KINROSS

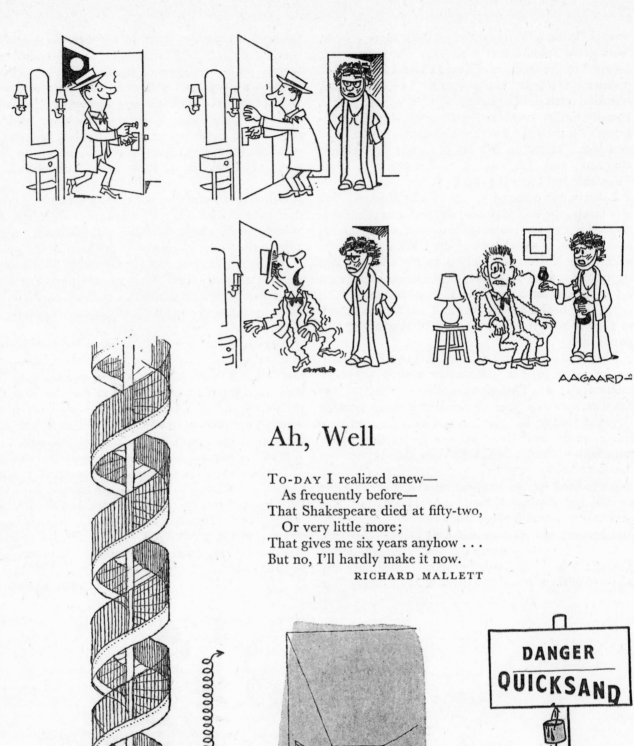

Ah, Well

TO-DAY I realized anew—
    As frequently before—
That Shakespeare died at fifty-two,
    Or very little more;
That gives me six years anyhow . . .
But no, I'll hardly make it now.
           RICHARD MALLETT

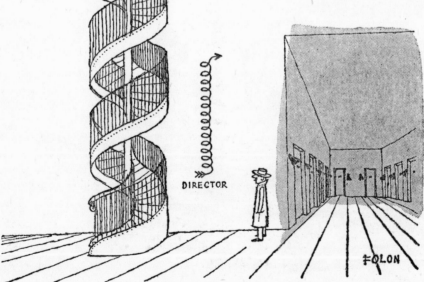

Les Eavesdroppeurs

RENÉ spent part of the summer with us in England. He was combining various pleasures with the duty of improving his English. His ear and eye are naturally quick. Sharply intent upon the behaviour of the English in public, he grew expert at overhearing stray fragments of dialogue. He rightly remarked that what is said spontaneously is likely to be a little revelation of national character. Going about with him we found ourselves beginning to use our eyes and ears somewhat as he did. We understand better now why he regards the manners of the English as bizarre.

It began near the sea, when we passed a young woman of the kind known as holidaymakers. She was trailing back sun-scorched from the beach, followed at a few paces by her son, a laggard of perhaps eight or nine. She turned and said something to him. He failed to hear it and said 'What?' She stopped as if struck by some missile, frowned, and said severely, 'Don't say "What?" Say "Pardon?" '

'C'est merveilleux!' cried René, or words to that effect. 'Is it then wrong to say "What?"?'

'Not at all,' we said. 'In fact many mothers, if their sons had said "Pardon?" would at once have said, just as crossly, "Don't say *Pardon?* Say *What?*" '

'Therefore what is right for some sons is not right for others? When I do not hear what a woman says to me, how am I to know when to say "What?" and when to say "Pardon?"?'

'Stick to "What?" ' we advised him.

'Very well, I will take your advice. But you have not told me why.'

There was nothing for it but to get him to read John Betjeman's *How to Get On in Society*, and then try to explain it to him.

'We are bound to confess,' we said, 'that it's all a matter of class-consciousness. Of course *we* don't mind if you call a serviette a serviette, especially as you're French.'

'Ah,' he said, 'and will it be all right if I call a spade a spade, as I am not English?'

This must have been a specimen of that Gallic wit one hears about.

'Here is a useful English phrase for you to learn,' I said. '*If you're so sharp you'll cut yourself.*'

The next day we saw two schoolgirls about to turn a corner. They seemed too mild looking to have come from St Trinian's. One was tallish, with darkish red hair and the pale complexion that goes with it; the other was meek-looking, with a neat pigtail. Just as they turned the corner Redhead stopped suddenly, glared at Pigtail and said in a shrill voice: 'Oh, you *horrible* thing! Oh, you *are* horrible! I'll *never* speak to you again!'

René clasped his hands together in ecstasy, and strained his ears to hear more as the two girls, having turned the corner, moved off side by side. No doubt Redhead had only been using a figure of speech, because, as the figures of the two girls receded, there was a renewed exchange of speech between them. Unfortunately none of us could catch a word of it.

René was almost amok with curiosity.

'But what could she have said? "*Horrible thing!*" Is that not a little strong? Do you think it was a personal remark—something about her looks, perhaps? "I think red hair is beastly," or something of that kind? Or do you think it was something improper?'

I may say that René's English accent is not perfect, and he pronounced this last word *improper*. Then he said, 'If I listen too much, you will call me, how-do-you-call-it, an *eavesdroppeur*.'

From that moment we have called the chance overhearing of other people's talk *eavesdroppant*, which after all is not much odder as a word than the one René applied to a rather rustic-looking wide-brimmed straw hat from British Guiana which my wife wore in the sun. She asked him how he liked it. He said politely that it was '*très folk-lore*'.

When René left us we did a short part of the train journey with him. As we waited on the platform I noticed that he moved surreptitiously nearer to an unobtrusive couple on a seat, a quiet, prosperous-looking couple. They were of advanced middle-age, both well dressed in grey.

'*Oh, quel eavesdroppeur!*' I murmured, wagging a finger at him.

'They have said nothing!' he muttered. 'Not one word! They have been too long married, isn't it? After the silver wedding, I suppose, one can find nothing more to say.'

The decorous couple got into the compartment next to ours. It was a first-class one, and as the morning was hot all the doors into the corridor were open. Soon after the train had started we heard the voice

'Darling, you look wonderful to-day.'

of the husband in the next compartment for the first time. It was a quiet, clear, gentlemanly, resigned, world-weary drawl. What it said was:

'By the way, you've got lipstick all over your face and all over your teeth.'

The reply was unhurried.

'Well, that's what comes of having to do everything in such a hurry, John.' Then on a slightly rising note: 'But I *can't* have!'

With infinite patience and resignation he replied:

'It's no good saying you *can't* have, Elspeth. You *have*.'

And with a resolute crackle *The Times* could be heard rising up before him to shut out the sight of her retouchings.

René was enchanted.

'But in France this would be impossible!' he cried. 'It is exquisite! *All oveur your face!*'

He then wanted to know about the name Elspeth, and tried in vain to pronounce it. Before he had made any progress it was time for us to get out.

'*Bon voyage*,' we said, as he leant out of the window, '*et bon eavesdroppant.*'

'Oh certainly,' he said. 'Little *pitcheurs* have long ears.'

WILLIAM PLOMER

'It's just like billiards.'

'*Good Lord—we forgot the onions!*'

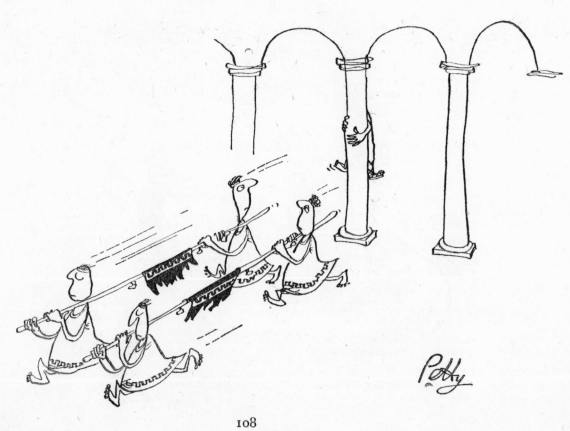

How I Done my Research

It is reported that the standard of English shown in papers at the recent entrance examination of the Westminster Medical School of the University of London bordered on illiteracy. In this connection we feel it essential to place before the world the first of a series of extracts, eventually to appear in The Lancet, *from a treatise by Dr P. Henbane, one of the most brilliant minds in the future of medical science, on his investigations into the cause and cure of the common cold.*

THIS chap X comes in to the Surgry on the Wensday all puffed up round the Eyes and Snuffling something terrible. What's to do? I says, so he says I'm all bunged Up and canot Breath proper. You have got a common cold, I says, and he says How can I get Releef?

This set me thinking, as I have often wondered about this Problem ever since I was a kid, as my Aunty was for ever Snuffling and spent a fortune on Hankys in her time and I was a great Faverite of hers. Come and see me the day after Tomorrow, I says, and in the meen time I will have a Think.

So anyway, on the Friday Mr X comes in again and his nose is Running and he has got a bit of a Temprature. Blimey, I says, it is coming on Bad, is it not? Yes, he says I feel done in and have lost the use of one Nostril. Let me have a look at your throte and everything, I says, so I gave him a thorough going over. There was free discharge of mucus and some Inflamation of the membranes of Nose Throte and Eyes and this was getting on to his Windpipe and Bronichal tubes through the Larynks.

Anyhow, I got hold of some of this Stuff I had mixed up, made out of a bit of camponicorum and some epthelmicus virus and I thought to myself, this might do the Trick so here goes. Because I had been having this Theery off and on for years, you see. It's all to do with Virus I don't care what Anyone says as what else can it be. Anyhow I stuck a bit of this up his nose and here and there and off he goes Home and I thought no more about it until the Monday.

What have you done to my Breething? he says on the Monday. Why? I says, what is up with you now? Blimey, he says, I canot hardly eat my Scoff in case I Choaks, and also my nose won't even run to give me releef. You have Bunged me Up worse than what I was on the Wensday, he says, and that stuff you have give me to snuff up smells Awful. Well, I says, this is very intresting. I think I am on the Right Track, I says to him. I know, he says, but my eyes keep on Running also, and my taste Buds have gone funny. It is your Cold that is doing that, I says, but the day will come when I will have a cure for it. All right, he says, I will be your Guinuea Pig, so I gets him down on the table and off with his Westcoat. You should have heard his Tubes, they were Cronhic.

Anyhow, to cut a long Story short, I mixes up a bit more of this here Virus and daubs some of it on to his Tonsills. What are you doing now? he says. I am trying out a new System, I says. He took it in good part, and the following Teusday in he comes again with his alm in a sling. Dear dear, I says, what has Occured to you at this juncture? I have fell down a kind of Man hole, he says, what with my eyes being Bunged Up I could not see proper where I was going, and Now look at me. Do not worry, I says, as one day there will be statues of you all over the place. I know that, he says, but I am wanting to get back to Work, as I do not desire my Mates to laugh at me and say sissy. Mr X, I says, I have just been struck with an Idea. Good, he says, what is it? I canot tell you Yet, as it must remain a Secret for the time been. You sit there, I says, and wait while I nip out for a bit more Stuff from the chemists.

This was on the Teusday. On the Friday I had a Sensational developement.

ALEX ATKINSON

The Authorship of Barrack Room Ballads

IT IS too late now to save the memory of Shakespeare from burglarious claims on his work put forward on behalf of so many writers, and now by the ghost of Marlowe. But, in order to prevent that kind of thing from happening again, I am collecting evidence to prove that the works of Rudyard Kipling were not written by Swinburne (supposed to have died in 1909) or by any Lord Chancellor.

Likely arguments that the future may raise in favour of Swinburne's authorship of *Barrack Room Ballads* and *Plain Tales from the Hills* would seem to be these: that Kipling was much too young, when these books first appeared, to have had time for the education necessary for the production of such masterpieces, whereas Swinburne about that time was entering his sixties. That Swinburne did not sign them himself is easily explained by a certain modesty to be found in all the work attributed to Kipling which was quite out of harmony with Swinburne's previous poems, so that he preferred to attribute *Barrack Room Ballads* to a different hand from that earlier one that was more at home with the roses and lilies of something a bit more erotic. And as these books dealt with India, whose sultry climate and mystery had evidently allured Swinburne's imagination, he ascribed their authorship to a young journalist who, as he must have chanced to find out, was at that time resident in India.

Subsequent to the year 1909, when Swinburne is supposed to have died, it would have been easy for almost any country gentleman to have concealed him in his house, and there have given him the opportunity of continuing the works which he signed with the name of Rudyard Kipling. Arundel Castle or Petworth, both in Sussex, would have been convenient places for such concealment, and are equally probable, though there are several other houses that might have served the purpose; but the indications that the place of concealment was somewhere in Sussex are very strong. And the absence of any typescript proving the contrary in the tombs of the late owners might be taken as support for the Swinburnians in the Swinburne-Kipling controversy.

But, whatever the house in which Swinburne was concealed after 1909, posterity will be sure to point out that there was nothing extraordinary in this concealment, since, before there was any suggestion of his disappearance in 1909, it is clearly recorded that Theodore Watts-Dunton had practically concealed him at Putney for many years, and may have, indeed, continued to do so in that same house after 1909, if he was not concealed in Sussex, whither Swinburne's poetic imagination may have roamed from Putney, as it had previously done to India.

The evidence that I am collecting to refute this theory, whenever it may be put forward, is strong, but I had been wondering how best to present it to posterity. I have now discovered, however, by examining all records of the present and past which deal with such matters, that the almost invariable method of presenting such proofs is to do so by cryptograms concealed in a verse. My proof therefore that Swinburne did not write Kipling's best known poem, from which it may be presumed that he wrote none of the works of Kipling, is contained in the following sonnet; and all those who have ever proved that the works of Shakespeare were written by the Lord Chancellor of his day will be sufficiently familiar with such proofs to examine the first letter of each line of my sonnet, which I hope will prove to posterity that Swinburne did not write Kipling.

SONG BEFORE TEA-TIME
by
A. S.

In the dull gray fogs of the old year's ending
  (Drip and drizzle till gutters freeze),
In woods forlorn with their branches bending
  Down at will of a bitter breeze,
Not a bird of them all is sending
  Out his song from the stricken trees
To tell us Spring is on slow feet wending
  Whence she loiters by southern seas.

Red on hearths is the oak-log's ember
  Inly glowing where ash is gray
To warm our hands that have lost December,
  Even to find a bleaker day,
In the cold of which we can scarce remember,
  Far though Spring, she is on her way.

LORD DUNSANY

The Bandit

A LONG time ago I bought a bicycle and crossed the Channel and raced the dying winter to Perpignan. At the Spanish frontier the drums of spring already sounded, and a wind from Africa, hot as a fabulous brothel, blew through the customs shed. Further and further south I went. 'Seville?' I cried to people on the road. 'Seville,' they cried back, pointing, and slowly I reached young leaves and the cool swoop of arches and time sleeping like a dog in the sun. Then I climbed a hill, and orange blossom, like a perfume of ancient empires, was in the breeze. I saw an old man scratching the soil with a hoe. 'Seville?' I shouted. 'Seville,' he cried back, and suddenly, as though he knew the urgency, took me by the hand and ran with me to the top of a hill and I looked down. Seville lay below me like an exquisite ivory chess set.

Two years later I returned to Seville, and stayed in a derelict inn across the Guadalquivir. In the distance I could see the elegant finger of the Giralda point to the sky. The inn was kept by a retired bull-fighter, who had three sons, Luis, Pedro and Miguel. Luis and Miguel were bullfighters, Pedro was a foot-baller. 'Praise be to God,' said his mother. Pedro had bulging calves and knew everything about English cup ties. 'To fight bulls is not a thing of education,' he told me. Though Luis and Miguel lacked the modern education of the bull, they had more charm. Particularly Miguel. Miguel was a very young man who was just beginning to fight terrible old bulls in obscure villages. 'They know Latin and Greek,' he told me, 'and are as big as cathedrals.'

He was keen on his art, and used to practise cloak and mulet with a wild boar, called the Bandit, which he kept chained up to an olive tree near the inn. The Bandit was growing a fine pair of tusks and ripped Miguel's trousers to ribbons as he practised with half veronica and went in for the kill with a wooden sword. In the evenings, when the inn was crammed with gossips, Miguel unchained the Bandit and it wandered in through the door and rooted among the tables. Everyone screamed and jumped up on chairs, and devout old women prayed to various regional Virgins, and manzanilla and anis ran all over the floor.

One day Miguel came into my room, which was crammed with a lot of rather bored canaries, and said, 'To-morrow we go to the carnival. You must get yourself a typical costume and we will hire a carriage and join the procession.' I borrowed a black Cordoba hat, a white waistcoat and stove-pipe trousers. 'We wear masks,' said Miguel, 'and speak in high falsetto. Nobody speaks in their own voice during the carnival.' The next day we got into the carriage, and there were two gipsy girls in it called Consolation and Concepcion, and we joined a stream of other carnival carriages and screamed at each other in falsetto voices and posed as typically as possible. For about an hour the carnival was a gracious, quite elegant affair, and people screamed and threw flowers at the carriages, but later on everyone got drunk and they started throwing earth and I lost my hat and Miguel bashed a man over the head with a guitar. 'This is a good carnival,' screamed Miguel. 'Now we'll get out of the carriage and walk down the street and sweep everyone off the pavement. Consolation and Concepcion, walk behind us.' We did this and later found ourselves in a cake shop near the Sierpes. 'I must go,' said Miguel, 'and feed the Bandit.' After he had left, some young men came in and screamed at us and we threw cakes at each other, while the proprietor bowed and totted down each item on a bill. After the cake fight was over one of the young men waved

magnificently and left. 'The Marquis is paying,' said the proprietor with another bow. 'He never misses the carnival cake fight, does the Marquis. A proper young señorito.'

When I returned to the inn, covered with cream, it was night and the fish were leaping like knives in the river. I started to make for my room, when I heard a terrible snuffling and froze where I stood. 'Keep still,' cried the voice of Miguel, now deep and natural. 'Don't move an inch. He will probably only sniff at you. Behave like a tree.' I listened to the snorting approach of the Bandit and behaved like a tree, though a trembling one. It zig-zagged through the night and nosed to my feet, suspicious and bristling. After ten minutes of toppling terror I heard it lunge away into the night and I tiptoed to my room and collapsed into the bed. Later I left Spain, and Miguel saw me off at the station. 'You will come back to Seville,' he shouted. 'I will come back,' I shouted back. 'For the carnival,' shouted Miguel in a suddenly high voice. 'For the carnival,' I screamed back in falsetto, and the train left and I tried never to let the magic go; but it went, petering out among prams and privet and red brick crescents in the rain.

Twenty years later, grey and not so near the stars, I found myself back in Seville. I got myself a carriage and drove through the old flower-studded streets, the barrio of Santa Cruz, the Alcazar, and then across the river to the inn of my honeymoon. A plump woman served me with a manzanilla. She looked at me with curiosity and said suddenly 'You are the man in the photograph?' She pointed to a glass case which contained pictures of bullfighters, and in the very centre a photograph of Miguel, myself, Concepcion and Consolation and El Sordo driving away for the carnival. I sat down and drank many manzanillas, and the Giralda glittered in the distance like a vision. The woman was Pedro's wife. 'His father and mother are dead and so are Luis and Pedro. Miguel will be here this evening. I will tell him you are here.'

I returned in the evening. It was already dark and I paused at the broken down gate of the inn. In the distance I could hear the tinkle and rumble of a guitar, and it woke a sleeping nerve. I walked forward and suddenly froze. Something was snuffling and snorting under the trees, I stood absolutely still for twenty minutes and then, as the creature got closer, I shouted 'Miguel'!

All the lights of the inn went on, and a tall dark man came running out, laughing, to embrace me. A little way away, staring up at me with minute, suspicious eyes, was a tiny pig.

ANTHONY CARSON

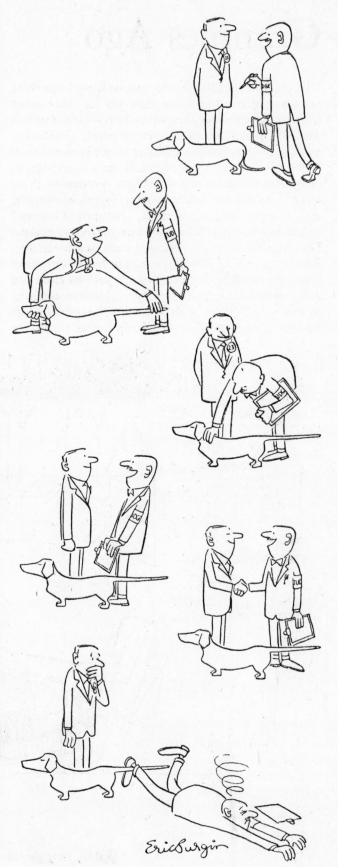

113

Grannies Ago

You will surely know them, out walking in park or cedarn garden, parasoled thus yet in some cases propped cropped at chromium bars—then a salted almond caught like amber among pearly dentures—steatopygous in old black silks or trimly tweeded with a dry martini under the belt and the cut-and-thrust of old Nick himself—these elderly women of three score years and ten, grannies, short for grandmothers, and, as some of us like to think, also units of history?

Yardsticks, yearsticks, they bring History, evasive beast, to life: for taking seventy years as a mean age, is it not revealing that if you add so few as only *three* grannies together, lay them gently end to end, you are plumb in the middle of the eighteenth century, in the '45 rebellion, with Mme de Pompadour just beginning and the French Revolution as far in the future as A.D. 2000 is to us? Only three of these grannies!

While two grannies, a simple brace of old ladies, as young as they feel, lands you in the Battle of Waterloo. Only five grannies ago and it is the Gunpowder Plot, with gentlemen in lace plus-fours and torture an ordinary pleasure. And just take the lives of ten grannies, just ten laughing little old ladies linking hands, and you are expecting the birth of Giotto, the signing of the Magna Carta is within recent memory, and Marco Polo is packing for the East. But wait! Only a hundred grannies ago, in what some people are pleased to exaggerate as 5000 B.C., the first Pharaoh ascended the throne. *That*—within the lifetimes of only a mere hundred little old lavender-and-lacers!

How close they bring us to the Past, no more so distant! What a short thing their long little lifetimes make of history! How they mock our clumsy and illusionary digits—1265 indeed, 5000 B.C.! What

'*Ah well, bang goes the Concours d'Elégance.*'

foolish figures are these compared with such flesh and blood erections of parasol and silk, bustling with em-bustled life, fleet-foot châtelaines of the flashing years! And as for that other unit, the 'generation', as absurd a conception as it is elastic—for is it really thirty years? Why not twenty-five? Or possibly forty? —how simply these grannies dispose of all such in-decision! No, we may forget such arbitrary nonsenses —and rather remember that the failing eye of one granny actually looks into the first lively intelligence in the baby eyes of the granny-to-be, they are con-nected, they know each other, history rocks history in its arms, history throws a ball through history's cucumber frame, history smacks history and is for-ever remembered . . . the living link is forged.

About a dozen grannies ago Harold caught it in the eye at Hastings, and . . . but I am interrupted . . . someone has said 'Why not grandpas?' Unfair to the ladies! I am sorry. But the matter is easily answered. It is simply that 'grandpa' is too bewildering, too bumpy a word—and for me at least it is confusing, it conjures up too easily a different unit altogether, some whilom unit of Balkan currency, enormous coloured notes of 1,000 *pas* each gambled away by fiercely skirted colonels of *evzones* throughout the night of long moustaches before the trams bell once more a greeting to the bright Athenian dawn. . . .

But, you say, there are granny-knots? My sole riposte: I do not *feel* them so much. It is a matter of taste: we are creatures of our own experience, no more than the sum total of our acquired sensibilities. And it is a sum total of grannies, I repeat, that makes history. Lay these obliging old dears end to end and top to toe, and time contracts with a true elastic bang: besides, this could not be done with men, they die too early, the ladies hold the ashes of longevity; and indeed, if your sensuality descends to the slide-rule, and you would prefer some higher annual unit like seventy-seven to the proposed mean old age, you may be sure the ladies would oblige, and then a thousand years must seem only the shorter.

'Not three grannies have passed since serfs were sold with the British collieries . . .' 'Once upon a granny . . .' brisks the old fairy tale. 'Shakespeare? Quite a modern. Roughly five grannies old.'

It is a humbling thought. And it becomes doubly remarkable when one realizes that only the shorter stretches of time are beneath the measurement of these indefatigables, the putative unit refuses such as a trifling fifty years. We do not, without embarrass-ment, like to say 'Within a granny'. Here is an intimacy that deters, one is faced with putting one's finger on the particular nook within the granny.

Where, exactly, *is* fifty years? The decent finger hesi-tates, it flinches to point—perhaps *there* is fifty years? —at where the elastic of lilac drawers binds tight the wholesome grey wool stocking. The waist? Too reminiscent of girlhood evenings down some long-lost Lover's Lane—not apt at all. The locket on her breast? But that contains her own grandmother's hair! Such multiplicity confounds. And the least we want to do is to strip our grannies bare as those veinous charts of the muscled body that hang on the walls of medical schools. Not that. No, leave them unintruded, in bombazine and bonnet, isolated figures on the Broad Walk, figures to be observed with lowered eye and bated breath. For there strides an Age.

And see—that Old Ladies' Outing, that chara-banc-full of porty dears a hundred strong! *That's* Ancient Egypt! A beanfeast of grannies . . . and you are back with the bricks and the straw and the vague possibility of perhaps one day a pyramid or two . . . a few more beanfeasts, and there's Neanderthal and Peking Granny: one more beanfeast, and there are not any grannies at all, the gun has not gone for the human race, one notices a face too furry beneath the flowered bonnet, no mittened fingers but oh such a long prehensile tail waves from the window its Union Jack, and above the driver's seat appear, backwards, tell-tale letters, **OOƧ**.

WILLIAM SANSOM

115

At the theatre with Ronald Searle

Dorothy Tutin as
Joan in *The Lark*

Donald Pleasence in *Misalliance*

Paul Scofield as *Hamlet*

Nigel Patrick as *The Remarkable Mr. Pennypacker*

Athene Seyler
as Mrs. Malaprop in *The Rivals*

Yves Robert as Gérard Barbier
in *Histoire de Rire*

John Gielgud as Benedick and Peggy Ashcroft as Beatrice
in *Much Ado About Nothing*

Roger Livesey in *Misalliance*

Irene Worth as Alcestis in *A Life in the Sun*

At the Show

JOHNNIE RAY AT THE LONDON HIPPODROME

'You folks,' says Mr RAY in a voice scraped raw with song, 'are more generous to me than I deserve'. The house shrieks indignantly, because this is practically abdication; but finding that its idol is only introducing his tribute to the band (not only very wunnerful musicians but each one my very dear friend') it roars

obedient acclaim, and the band rise to their feet with the sulky air of men who know that they are only another man's gimmick. For Mr RAY's gimmick is to affect a touching humility before the gifts divinely bestowed on him. This is no easy trick for an extrovert-plus, but he performs it creditably. As he sings, his large bony fingers grope for confidence among the spotlight's motes, or nervously smooth the pockets of his costly dinner-suit; his gangling frame folds into the diffident attitudes of a lady companion anxious to please an exacting employer: in approaching a high note he is the schoolboy cricketer praying to hold a vital catch: he will often hesitate before a phrase, gathering himself, uncertain whether his technique is equal to the task of interpretation. To give him his due, such phrases as 'Rapture supreme, what a heavenly scheme' take some interpreting through an unmuted seven-piece brass section and an audience of pigs going to the slaughter.

As the evening wears on he gathers a little self-esteem; his gestures open out; he falls on a knee and thumps the stage; his hair-do collapses; he begins to get his teeth almost literally into his material, worrying the lyrics like a terrier with an old boot, biting off the sugary phrases as if they were sticks of seaside rock. In an atmosphere of rising hysteria he gradually expands towards vocal and physical contortions which he knows from experience will drop a spark into the emotional powder-barrels out front—an arm thrown up, an interpolated exclamation, a sudden spasmodic shake of the head. The screams mount, the band blasts. Those who would like to leave dare not, for fear of lynching.

His secret is dark, powerful and obscure. He lays claim, by implication chiefly, to some sense of soul ('Wanna walk an' talk with my Lord,' he bawls, tousled and sweating), and perhaps to his particular audience his shallows of the spirit seem like deeps. On the other hand, the screamers and shriekers and long, ecstatic moaners, as he drags out tormentedly, 'a favourite of my Mom and Dad's,' are clearly getting a separate satisfaction out of their own be-

118

haviour. In fact so much of the performance is contributed from the auditorium that it is as hard to assess its merits as it is to explain its success. On the last score, the ostentatiously-worn deaf aid should not perhaps be over-looked. It hints at a frailty bravely overcome, and stirs all kinds of half-realized compassions, particularly in those who forget that deaf aids can be had in much less conspicuous forms nowadays.

J. B. BOOTHROYD

At the Opera

LA TOSCA AT COVENT GARDEN

THE TOSCA, RENATO TEBALDI, has a big voice of variable quality which, at best, dazzles and stuns rather than seduces. Her *Vissi d'arte* stopped the show. In Miss TEBALDI's acting there was no hint of the imperious, impulsive diva, no sweeping on and off like an adored typhoon. This Tosca was a thoroughly nice young woman. My heart bled for her in the torture scene. I wanted to see her rescued and getting on with potting ham and pruning roses at the place she and her stockbroker husband have, for sure, somewhere up the river.

The unusual merit of GOBBI's Scarpia is that it makes hay of type-casting and flies fruitfully in the face of nature. GOBBI has frank, pleasant, open features and a personality to match. Nothing could be imagined less like a torturing police chief. Puccini and Sardou would have given him up as hopeless at a glance. Yet . . . Nature's handicaps were cancelled by sheer acting power—and fine, intelligent singing.

DON GIOVANNI AT SADLER'S WELLS

The *Giovanni* of the Carl Rosa Company was held together by a single personality, in this case that of JOHN HEDDLE NASH, a young baritone who carries a distinguished name with confident stage bearing, easy gesture, a gleaming smile and the capacity to stand still without looking a fool. To these assets add an agreeable voice agreeably used. The total still falls short of Giovanni as imagined by da Ponte and Mozart, a creature of brimstone and high breeding who leaves ninety-nine baritones out of a hundred at the starting-gate. Mr NASH is not to be blamed for being among the ninety-nine.

Nor is it any fault of his that the crucial Supper scene misfired. Instead of being liveried and on the

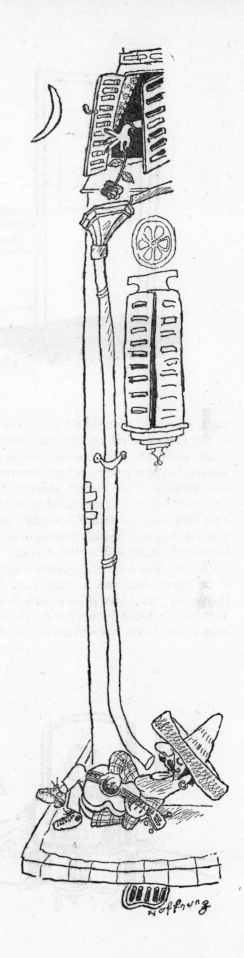

On the Air

I NEVER cease to marvel at the technique of the BBC's sporting commentators. They manage to inject some kind of excitement into the dullest interludes. The football commentator forces his voice to a mad strangled crescendo as play nears the penalty area and yells 'Goal! No, it isn't!' as soon as a centre-forward leaps to head from a corner-kick. The racing commentator sees a 'procession' as a nerve-shattering struggle and becomes incoherent to order during the last two furlongs. But the boys who really earn their fees are the ingenious gasbags who convert rain-sodden turf and waterproof covers into verbal thrills. At Manchester (yes, Manchester) the other week rain stopped play during the third round of the Davis Cup Match between Great Britain and India, and a certain commentator waded in with a pulsating account of the new plastic covers. Then the rain eased and he became delirious in the attempt to suggest mounting excitement as the ground-staff slipped smoothly into action. 'The whole job is being tackled with incredible, almost military, precision. The gleaming covers are being rolled up like long green sausages and the pools of water are *disappearingasifbymagic*! And now the covers are being carried away . . . one, two, *three*, FOUR, FIVE! And not a drop of water has been allowed to spoil this fine court. Well, there's just a little, yes, I can see a small pool, a *very* small pool, but it's so close to the net that it'll cause no trouble . . .'

It was a wonderful performance, dramatic, inspiring, intoxicating, When it was all over, and play was resumed, I felt like a wet rag.

BERNARD HOLLOWOOD

stage, Giovanni's household musicians stayed down in the orchestra pit and tootled their quotes from *Figaro* and other contemporary hits so grossly that it was hard to hear a word either Giovanni or Leporello was singing. The Statue entered like a frigid, aggrieved butler who is minded to hand in his notice. The limp way he took Giovanni's proffered hand made it clear that he didn't mean to be won over by a lot of last-minute smarm, thank you.

The tempi of ARTHUR HAMMOND again made some of us stare, start and mutter. . . . Evidently Mr HAMMOND has ideas of his own how Mozartian 'ornament' should be rendered. There should have been a note in the score to steel us against the shock.

CHARLES REID

Booking Office

THE UNKNOWN PRIME MINISTER: *Robert Blake*

IT IS difficult to be interested in Bonar Law; and though Mr Robert Blake is skilful, witty and scholarly in his treatment of the subject, Bonar Law's interest (if he had any) continues to be elusive. Such remarks of his as are quoted by Mr Blake are banal; his writings have about them a flatness which makes Mr Attlee seem a kind of Montaigne; his very appearance suggests a mayor, or possibly a lord mayor, about to beat the bounds of a not very distinguished borough. I read somewhere, or heard, that a favourite joke of his was, when he knocked out his pipe, to pretend that he thought it was someone knocking at the door and to shout out: 'Come in!' This macabre episode, it would appear, never lost its relish for him.

Yet Bonar Law became leader of the Conservative Party, and in due course Prime Minister, and obviously was endowed with, or was helped by Lord Beaverbrook to exercise, quite a lot of native political cunning. Mr Blake admirably describes the various machinations whereby he first pushed himself forward, leaving Long and Austen Chamberlain to fall neatly one on each side of the chair they both thought they were going to sit down in; then joined Lloyd George to oust Asquith and then led the Conservatives in ousting Lloyd George. All the same it has to be admitted that, despite Mr Blake's meticulously engaging efforts, Bonar Law remains an unknown Prime Minister because one comes to feel there was nothing to know about him.

For me, however, the fascination of Mr Blake's book lay elsewhere. One of the most bizarre enterprises of the age is the manner in which Lord Beaverbrook is supervising the publication of contemporary history to ensure that his own rôle is suitably presented. His method is, first, to acquire the requisite Papers; then to find a suitable scribe, and, finally, when the book is out, to use his newspapers to boost it with full-throated ease.

It is always fascinating to see how a man as unusual as Lord Beaverbrook sees himself and his activities. One of the fallacies of life is to suppose that a person's view of himself conforms to that of his fellows—that, for instance, Stalin used to wake up in the morning and remember that he had murdered most of his friends and associates; or that Gladstone went about haunted by the feeling that he was a portentous old humbug. Not at all. Stalin, I am sure, always thought of himself as a particularly good and faithful friend, and Gladstone imagined himself gifted with a charm which would have made Byron sick with envy.

So with Lord Beaverbrook. He has lived long in this wicked world, and, through the possession of wealth, newspapers and useful associations, has made himself a person of importance. We all know really quite a lot about him. I was therefore particularly diverted by one episode in *The Unknown Prime Minister*. It relates to the manner in which Lord Beaverbrook was ennobled. Although, one gathers, Lord Beaverbrook's efforts to get Asquith out and Lloyd George in were actuated solely by his affection for Bonar Law and concern for the public interest, it appears that there was some sort of understanding that, when Lloyd George formed his government, Lord Beaverbrook would be President of the Board of Trade. So confident was Lord Beaverbrook that this bargain would be honoured that he told his constituents at Ashton-under-Lyne to expect a by-election (in those days M.P.s who accepted office had to fight by-elections). Imagine, then, the shock to his trusting nature when it turned out that Lloyd

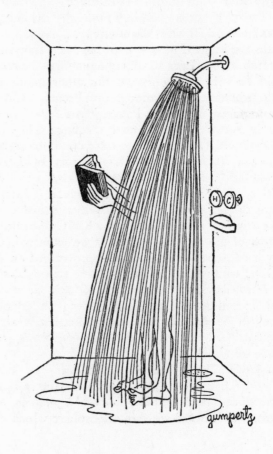

George proposed to put Sir Albert Stanley at the Board of Trade, and offer Lord Beaverbrook only a minor office or a peerage. He (Lord Beaverbrook), Mr Blake writes, 'was not anxious to leave the House of Commons. On the other hand it was a very convenient way out of an embarrassing predicament over his constituency, and would save him the humiliation of explaining why there would not after all be any by-election. He decided that he would accept.'

MALCOLM MUGGERIDGE

DU CÔTÉ DE CHEZ TIGI-DWT

MISS POTTER (like Jane Austen, she surely demands this perennial title of respect) has been translated into many languages, but *Peter Rabbit* is the first of her books to appear in Italian. Like Proust, alas, her peculiar qualities are but ill-suited to the language of Dante and Leopardi:

'*C'erano una volta quattro coniglini, che si chiamavano*
    Saltino,
    Saltarello,
    Fiocchetto,
    e Pierino . . .'

What, one asks oneself, has happened to Flopsy, Mopsy and Cottontail? Transformed, apparently, into a team of Italian acrobats; but why the change of sex? It is all very disquieting...

I do not know if Miss Austen has been translated into Italian, but I can hardly imagine that the result would be very felicitous. On the other hand, she would probably go well enough into French—and so, as it happens, does Miss Potter. *Pierre Lapin* triumphantly survives the channel crossing: Flopsaut, Trotsaut and Queue-de-Coton are credible enough, and even Mr MacGregor has a sort of horrid plausibility ('*Vite! Vite! Dépêchez-vous! Voici Mr MacGrégor!*'). *Jeannot Lapin, Poupette à l'Epingle, Jérémie Pêche-à-la-Ligne*—all these preserve the flavour of the original, with an added pinch of Gallic salt. In matters of gastronomy, as might be expected, the French editions tend to be an improvement on the English: thus, Mrs Rabbit (in *Pierre Lapin*) '*s'en va chez le boulanger, acheter une miche de pain bis et cinq brioches*'; and the 'roasted grasshopper with ladybird sauce' (in *Jeremy Fisher*) assumes an impressive air of *la haute cuisine* when rendered as '*rôti de sauterelle, sauce Bête-à-Bon-Dieu.*'

In *Jemima Puddle-Duck* (*Sophie Canétang*) the Gallic influence becomes almost embarrassingly pronounced, and the story of Sophie and *le gentleman aux favoris roux* is infused with an atmosphere which can only be described as *risqué*, if not positively *louche*. Sex—or something uncommonly like it—rears its ugly head: '*Comme je regrette,*' says the foxy-whiskered gentleman to poor, innocent Sophie, '*que vous soyez obligée de retourner chez vous pour y passer la nuit*'; and later he adds (in even more sinister accents): '*Je désire vous offrir un festin. Permettez que nous ayons un petit dîner en tête-à-tête.*' *Petit dîner*, indeed!

I have never, I regret to say, attempted to learn Welsh; but were I ever to succeed in mastering that barbaric and rebarbative tongue my favourite reading would not, I fear, be the Mabinogion or the Black Book of Carmarthen, but those modern (and perhaps more approachable) classics, *Hanes Dili Minllyn* and *Hanes Meistres Tigi-Dwt*. Nor do I know Dutch; but it would surely be worth learning if only to read *Twee Stoute Muisjes* or *Jeremias de Hengelaar*.

And when, by the way, will Miss Potter be translated into the language of Pushkin, Gogol and Turgenev? *Tovarich Piotr* and the *kulak* Gregor Gregorovich would surely go down well behind the Iron Curtain.

JOCELYN BROOKE

'*Don't expect too much—this is my first launching.*'

The Absolute (or Perfected) Chairman

JUST as we are each supposed to have one novel in us, so anyone who has appeared on a public platform has his little mite of experience to contribute to an understanding of the enigma of chairmen.

Why are chairmen so discussed? Why has thesis after thesis been written to explain what goes on in the chairman's mind?

The answer is, I think, that chairmen are subject to the temptations of all men who, even for a few moments, have absolute power. They are tempted to think that they can attain absoluteness of chairmanship, and this is because chairmen instinctively know that they have an aim which is more realizable on this earth than most other human aims. The aim is, of course, quite simply to cut the ground from under the feet of any particular speaker whom any particular chairman is introducing to any particular audience, so as to render what he has to say—and perhaps even his entire *persona*—unnecessary and superfluous.

The old style tactics of chairmen were all of the bulldozing kind. For instance, the chairman might give the lecturer's own lecture before he could get a word in edgeways; or he could give a different lecture arriving at conclusions contradicting everything the speaker had to say; or he could deliver a lecture on the lecturer, annihilating him with politeness. But such methods have the disadvantage of taking more time than modern audiences will sit through.

So the modern chairman usually begins with some original and disarming quip such as 'Chairmen, like children, should be seen and not heard.' Or 'The best chairmen disappear the fastest.' Or—if this could be contorted into sense—something on these lines: 'Of chairmen, like chairs, the least said soonest mended.'

In the age of jet propulsion there is a feeling that the chairman is a swordsman who must thrust swiftly and be done. What he, above all, needs to know is the most exposed weak places in the speaker. From experience I know that my own disadvantages are obvious. There is my name, which can easily be confused with Spencer or Spenser; and my reputation, which can be confounded by substituting the names of those colleagues with whom it is usually linked—Auden, MacNeice, Day Lewis.

At first sight it might seem that these openings are too obvious. Do they not reflect back a bit on the ignorance of the chairman? It all depends on how they are used.

The fascination of the chairman's business is to toy with ignorance, to wound and then extricate himself from responsibility for his weapon. So I give top marks to the chairman who introduced me with the remark that he was not going to fall into the trap that almost any other chairman would fall into—of calling me Mr Auden—and then wound up by saying: 'And now, ladies and gentlemen, I call upon Mr Auden to speak.'

The only example I have encountered of indubitably absolute chairmanning was an adroit use of the rather risky (from the chairman's point of view)

Spender-Spencer confusion. The stroke of genius with which the chairman was able to use this to rout me completely was owing to the fact that his own name happened to be Spencer. It was in Harvard in 1947 that the late Professor Spencer introduced me to read my poems. He made a brief, witty and informative *exposé* which he concluded by saying: 'And now I shall invite Professor Spencer to read his poems'. (He happened, by the way, to write poems himself.) A roar went up which my reading did little to assuage.

Probably techniques as skilled as this are only to be found at the great centres of culture—Oxford and Cambridge and Harvard. Any travelling lecturer will observe that in the outer rings of his circuit a provincial governor's Pontius Pilate attitude pertains among chairmen, as they wash their hands of the highbrows. To quote from my Journal, in which I note such things:

My chairman was a solicitor, a nice man, who provided an excellent meal, and, after the lecture, drinks. He introduced me by saying that he would be perfectly frank about his ignorance of the work of one he had never heard of until he was told to take the chair at this lecture. He had been informed that Mr S. was a poet, but that didn't get him any further, because he had never in his whole life read a line of poetry, having many other things to do. He had got one of Mr S's books out of the Public Library (*laughter*), where it happened to be, and as he didn't have time to read it, he had given it to the wife; but the wife had told him this very morning at breakfast (he hadn't seen her since breakfast) that she couldn't make head or tail of it (*laughter*).

There is a between-stools, British Council variant of this. British Council officials are, I suppose, a kind of bridge between highbrow and lowbrow worlds, and thus all their skill and tact goes into making the lowbrows feel that they are uncivilized, and the highbrows that they are oppressive monsters thrust upon ordinary real people. I quote from *Ibid*:

The British Council official who met me at the station explained that my lecture was to be introduced by a Lady Alderman. 'To be perfectly frank with you, old man, I told her that she'd most certainly be bored with your lecture, so I suggested she might take her leave directly after she'd made the introduction, which I offered to write for her. But, believe me or not, some of these Labour Aldermen are perfect bricks and prepared to go through with anything. You'll be pleased to hear that she said: "If it's my duty to stay, I stay".'

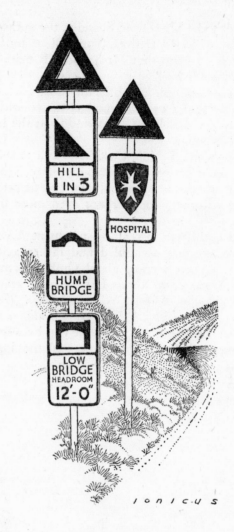

IONICUS

And stay she did. After saying her piece, she moved off the platform, sat in the front row directly opposite where I was standing, and went bang off to sleep.

Lord Pakenham's way of taking the Chair, as I once experienced it, I cannot attempt to classify, though it is very nearly an example of Absolute and Perfect Chairmanning. Yet there is a kind of ambiguousness about this example which does not permit one to know whether it was a pat on the shoulder or a knock-out blow. Some pats on shoulders are, I suppose, knock-out blows. Here is a rough paraphrase, as I remember it, of his introducing my lecture on Impressions of Germany, shortly after the end of the war:

'Ladies and gentlemen, a good many of you who have heard that Mr Spender is going to speak here to-night will have surmised that the person to address you is Mr J. A. Spender, the former editor of *The Westminster Gazette*; others, better informed, will have thought it to be Mr Harold Spender, the author of a biography of Lloyd George. You will be much relieved now to learn that Mr Spender is neither his uncle nor his father.'

Copying these words out for the third time, I feel little doubt that they fulfil most of the conditions I laid down for Absolute Chairmanship at the beginning of this paper.

Although not, I think, classifiable as a Pakenham Special, the experience at Amabel College (Ohio) of a poet I know was equally difficult to fit into any ordinary category, and perhaps even more undermining.

Lukas Quill was to read his poems at A.C. The whole college was assembled and rather agitated. Half the girls were crazy about Quill's poems, the other half was crazy about Lukas's photograph on the end-wrapper of Oscar Williams' *Major Treasures of Minor Modern Poetry*. I don't know whether it was a nervous endeavour to bridge the gap between this photograph and Lukas Quill in the flesh that inspired the Lady President and Lady Chairman, but this is what she said:

'For many semesters we have studied poetry at Amabel College. We know the names of so many many poets, and cherish them, some of them immortal, others of them, like Mr Lukas Quill sitting over there, still, happily, among us. For to-day we are greatly greatly privileged, we have a real live poet here amongst us—a poet who has written poems which appear under his own name—Lukas Quill—in anthologies in our own college library. Oh, isn't it just thrilling to look at Mr Lukas Quill sitting over there, and to think that he has flesh and parts like all the rest of us!'

This unmanned Lukas Quill as effectively as speaker has ever been made to wish he was extinct by Lady Chairman. He delivered his reading in a way the girls regarded as poetically characteristic—sheltered behind the barricade of the lecturer's table, which he had turned over on its side for that purpose.

STEPHEN SPENDER

What is a private view for? Well, its object is to give the genuine art lover a chance to study the pictures quietly and peacefully and without distraction before the show is . . .

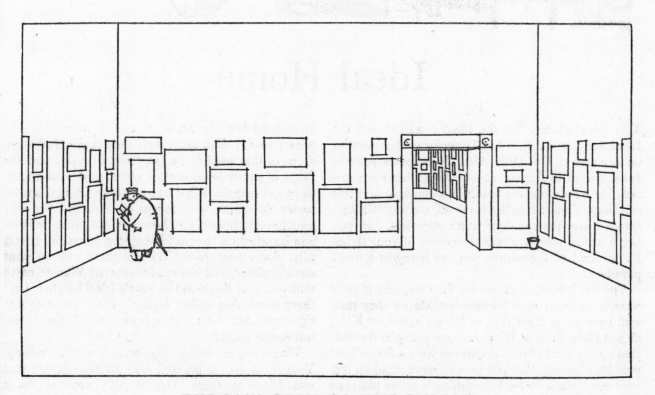

THROWN OPEN TO THE PUBLIC

Ideal Home

THE Ideal Home, like the Ideal Neckline and the Ideal Ball-point Pen, is Ideal only for twelve months, on account of the *Daily Mail*. It becomes *passé* in June, quaint in August, and in November somehow sad, like a lady playing tennis in a bandeau and lisle stockings. Finally handles come off, stuffing falls out, things warp, the car door won't stay shut, and you begin to feel uneasy about the colour of your slates. By the end of the winter you are living in a fool's paradise.

You can't be Contemporary for ever, and if your nursery curtains were Picasso last March they may well have to be Piper this, or Disney again, or Klee, or just plain striped. What are you going to do with that nearly oval platter decorated with a formalized pale blue herring that you used to serve salad on last year until you went back to dishing it up on plates so that nobody gets too many slices of egg? Platters with

formalized herrings on them are no more Contemporary to-day than those dear little Anne Hathaway cottages that used to be tea-cosies in 1927, and the shape of your television set is about as ideal as an upright gas-mantle. What are all these Chianti bottles under the stairs, with lumps of cork and two-way switches that have gone all loose? This coffee-bar that you installed on the roof last spring is looking pretty silly, don't you think? Why is there rust in your electric mixer, and bits of old custard? Who on earth told you your sink was this year's Ideal height? Isn't there something rather *nostalgic* about those square egg-cups? And what's that funny smell? You're not *still* eating pizza?

What you're doing, you see, is compromising. Your front door is painted acid yellow, because that was Ideal in 1946. This wobbly ash-tray on a chromium stalk came direct from the Exhibition of

1938. You have Ideal tin-openers from 1950, 1951 and 1953, although the one you actually use was invented in the year they first tinned beans. You've been fighting a losing battle and what you have on your hands now is not an Ideal Home at all. It's a hotch-potch.

You realize, of course, that if you keep on at this rate the most you can hope to achieve by the time you're too old to care anyway is a museum of memories? There you'll be, padding about in your current Ideal slippers, picking things up and putting them down and sighing. 'Ah, little green pottery hippo,' you will whisper, 'with crimson flowers dotted all over you—how Ideal you were way back in fifty-five! That was the year I broke my oboe, and Quare Times won the National.' There will be a carpet to evoke Eddie Cantor in *Whoopee!* A whisky glass decorated with a shingled nude (the last of the set) will recall the stirring days of Ramsay MacDonald and your primrose two-seater. You might even have things arranged room by room, decade by Ideal decade. 'Now here we have the 'thirties,' you might say, ushering people into some poky little hole near the spare bedroom, crammed with gaunt Ideal wardrobes and Van Gogh reproductions. Somebody will wind up the portable in the corner and you will all dance sadly to the music of Charlie Kunz, shuffling between dusty tasselled poufs, gaudy cocktail-shakers, and piles of vintage *Esquires*. Your history, your dreams, your Ideals, all pigeon-holed under one roof —and they wouldn't fetch fourpence at an auction.

It seems a pity. *Somebody* ought to try to keep in step.

ALEX ATKINSON

'*Will it wash?*'

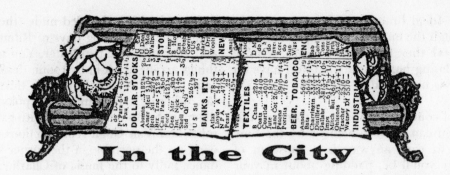

In the City

REVIVING TRENCHERMEN

SINCE 1946 the people of Britain have more than doubled their expenditure on food, and are now, in a nutritional sense, among the world's best eaters.

We continue to buy more food in spite of the fact that its price has climbed faster than that of any other item in the domestic budget. Since 1948 goods and services generally have become dearer by 25 per cent, but food prices are up by nearly 50 per cent. Manufactured household articles have risen by 20 per cent, clothing by 19 per cent, tobacco by 6 per cent, and alcoholic drink by 8 per cent. In 1946 we spent £1,816 millions on food: last year about £4,000 millions.

Our system of war-time and post-war controls, coupled with the feather-bedding ministrations of the Welfare State, turned the retail price structure upside down. Essentials—food, clothing and shelter—were made artificially cheap, and manufactured goods in the luxury and semi-luxury groups were made artificially dear by heavy indirect taxation and material shortages. The result was that the British worker lost his role as breadwinner and found inducement to work only in the promise of extra packets of cigarettes, bottles of beer, radio sets and the telly. His essentials were subsidized, his luxuries taxed, and in consequence our economic system was confronted for the first time with the problem of 'incentives'.

WALKIE-TALKIE

I GATHER that Mr Butler's very keen on profit-sharing—you know, workers' participation. Thinks it's the only way to prevent strikes.

You mean men wouldn't strike if they had a direct interest in the profits of their industry?

That's the idea. Shareholders never strike, not even P. & O. shareholders.

But wouldn't it be wiser to push ahead with automation and get rid of the workers altogether? No workers, no strikes.

And no purchasers either. No workers, no purchasing power.

Ah, but they could be kept on the payroll. That's the new American idea, isn't it? Ford Motors have given all their employees contracts guaranteeing them work or paid leisure for years.

And you think . . . ?

I don't think, I know. If we're going to have automatic, remote-control factories there's got to be some new way of pushing the money into circulation, and the Americans as usual have found the answer long before we've even begun to see the problem.

You're quite wrong about Ford's and the rest: their three-year contracts are an indication that the push-button factory is still light years away. Ford's are making sure of their labour for years to come.

I know the argument—even in the push-button factory there'll still be a need for men to push the buttons and make the buttons and organize reunions of displaced operatives. But I'm not impressed. Automation, not profit-sharing, is the logical way to improve industrial relations.

Well, I'm with Butler and companies like I.C.I., A.E.L., Rolls Royce, Tootals and Barclays. We must have incentives, and profit-sharing schemes provide the only incentives now acceptable to labour.

Bourgeois claptrap. Let me remind you that dividends on employees' shares are regarded as unearned income, and are subject to income tax at the higher rate, and that . . .

Golly, that reminds me! I've got an interview with an inspector-chap. Should have been there ten minutes ago.

MAMMON

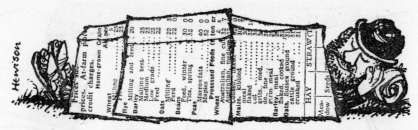

In the Country

THE HAMBLEYS kept a small shop in the village. I had often wondered how they managed, now I know. For they had few customers; not because their muddled and untidy emporium was not well stocked, it was; indeed it looked like the cache of an assiduous jackdaw, with ropes of leather bootlaces and bits of harness hanging from the ceiling above a counter piled with Swiss rolls and cans of paraffin in dangerous juxtaposition; but because they had failed to keep their stock up-to-date. They were both eighty, and some of their goods were almost as old. Their trade in carbide and night-lights was small after the electric mains were brought to the district. They continued to stock yeast and saffron although nobody in the village baked their own bread.

They were an independent but devoted couple, keeping themselves to themselves. We saw them only on Sundays when they passed by on the church parade, he looking like an elder statesman, wearing a starched dicky and a brown derby and buttoned boots; she in the style, fashion and deportment of the late Queen Alexandra. Last week she was found dead in the shop. That wasn't very surprising considering her age, but I was surprised to learn from the doctor that the old lady had in fact died of starvation. The very word came as a shock in an era that boasts that it has banished poverty.

'Their shop couldn't have brought them in more than a few shillings a week,' he told me.

'But they both had the Old Age Pension?' I protested.

'No they didn't. They refused to collect it.'

'Why?'

'Because, as he said yesterday, "Neither Mrs Hambley nor I wish to be dependent on charity either from the State or any other body." '

'Didn't you explain that it was their own money back again?'

'You can't explain to eighty,' he said. 'And what makes it most embarrassing for me is that they've insisted on paying me over £20 this year by refusing to go on the National Health. But once she went we had no alternative but to disregard the old man's pride, because there was nobody left to look after him.'

'What did you do?'

'We moved him to the workhouse yesterday. But it was no use. He died this morning. It wasn't grief but just the shame of accepting charity which killed him.'

More than Mr Hambley has died, a piece of England has died. Somebody should write its epitaph.

RONALD DUNCAN

On Wings of Song

I cannot say when it was that I first felt burgeon and stir within me the unshakable conviction that I was possessed of a glorious singing voice. Not just what people call a 'nice' voice, or even a 'fine' voice, but the kind of voice that bursts like a clarion call through a vast auditorium and ricochets off the back of the gallery—a voice that holds thousands spellbound.

Yes, *that* was my voice—when it had been properly trained, of course. I was fully conscious of my awful responsibility, although I had already been rejected as 'unrewarding' by four successive singing teachers without my confidence being in the slightest shaken. You see I'd read somewhere that, at the outset of *his* career, the young Richard Tauber had met with the same Philistine indifference. So I too serenely bided my time. In the privacy of the bathroom I continued to move vast audiences to rapture and tears.

Then by some fateful chance I came across Signor Donizetti Oreilly. Signor Oreilly had—to quote his prospectus—'sung in all the world's great opera houses and performed before most of the crowned heads of Europe'. It was the crowned heads that did it. Suddenly it flashed on me that here was a master worthy of his pupil. Fortunately he had just one vacancy left. Did he insist on auditions before accept-

ing pupils? 'Arra no not at all'—it was delightful to find that his dallyings with all those crowned heads had not diminished by one jot the native—was it Neapolitan?—brogue of the Signor Oreilly. 'Sure couldn't I tell,' he said, 'from the first syllable that dropped from your lips that it's a golden voice and a golden future you have in front of you.' That was all I wanted to hear. Already those thousands were swelling to tens of thousands, all of them moved . . . to rapture and tears.

Every Tuesday found me at the Signor's studio in East Croydon. And each day I came away feeling that I'd learnt something worth knowing. The first day I learnt that I was a counter-tenor, which was a little unsettling. Then it was decided that my tenor was heroic, which was more reassuring. Eventually I accepted the Signor's considered opinion that I was really a dramatic baritone with a *very* unusual range. Soon I realized that great singers are subject to the occupational maladies of cold feet and sore throats. To guard against these Oreilly had a small electric fire which he kept under the piano and a box of throat pastilles which he kept on top. The pastilles had a pleasant taste but the fire kept fusing, and, when it did, all work had to stop until it was mended.

We must have spent hours together under the piano tying bits of wire. Still, I felt that every time I was learning more and more about electric fires.

The Oreilly technique for voice-training was simple. We took the word 'laugh' with the long 'a' vowel and while the Signor pounded out the scale on the piano I stood in front of a mirror and let the liquid notes flow out. 'Laugh . . . la . . . a . . . a . . . augh . . . laa . . .' One must watch the throat carefully all the time—no strain, tongue in the right position, lips round and open wide. It was fascinating. After a while I got to know every little whim of my uvula. I even began to have wild ideas about specializing in ear, nose and throat.

And all the time I was practising. In the bedroom, in the office, in the street. Once in a bus, when I had struck an unusually high E sharp, an old lady got up and offered me her seat. My circle of acquaintances narrowed rapidly but I accepted that as the expected isolation of the great artist. Caruso, Chaliapin, they too had known solitude and the slavery of the perpetual scales.

It was during the forty-fourth lesson, when I could juggle with 'laugh, laugh, laugh' in every known permutation, that I began to have doubts. And so it was agreed that on the following Tuesday the Signor would have two experts along to pass judgment on my progress.

Well I remember the day. I reeled from the exhaustion of a last six days and nights spent with 'laugh . . . augh . . . augh'. I was keyed up to concert pitch. One look in the mirror and I recoiled. The panel of judges waited in silence. The Signor sat down at the piano. I was just clearing my throat for the very prototype of all tonic solfas when . . . phut! went the electric fire. Oreilly threw up his hands in despair and disappeared under the piano.

We never got the fire mended. From that day to this the glorious singing voice has been stilled. And yet sometimes, in the silent watches of the night, there appears before me a vast auditorium with a sea of upturned faces, all of them working convulsively and deeply, deeply moved . . . yes . . . to rapture and tears.

ROY BRADFORD

Sprod

Breakfast with Gerard Manley Hopkins

'Delicious heart-of-the-corn, fresh-from-the-oven flakes are sparkled and spangled with
sugar for a can't-be-resisted flavour.'—Legend on a packet of breakfast cereal

SERIOUS over my cereals I broke one breakfast my fast
    With something-to-read-searching retinas retained by print on a packet;
Sprung rhythm sprang, and I found (the mind fact-mining at last)
    An influence Father-Hopkins-fathered on the copy-writing racket.

Parenthesis-proud, bracket-bold, happiest with hyphens,
    The writers stagger intoxicated by terms, adjective-unsteadied—
Describing in graceless phrases fizzing like soda-siphons
    All things crisp, crunchy, malted, tangy, sugared and shredded.

Far too, yes, too early we are urged to be purged, to savour
    Salt, malt and phosphates in English twisted and torn,
As, sparkled and spangled with sugar for a can't-be-resisted flavour,
    Come fresh-from-the-oven flakes direct from the heart of the corn.

ANTHONY BRODE

'Now see here, Brother Matthew, are you going over my head?'

Dana Fradon

LIFT

FOURTH FLOOR
WORLITZ
SCHOOL
OF
LANGUAGES

ENGLISH
FRENCH

'Help! Au secours! Aiuto! Hilfe! Ajuda! Hailfe! Hjalp!'

Journal of a Fleet Street Psychologist

MONDAY. The usual end-of-the-year crop of journalists who feel they can't go on. It will be the same all week no doubt, with one or two Christmas Number complexes thrown in. Only three leader-writers this morning, however, and two of them were straightforward 'brooks no delay' cases.[1] The third was quite inarticulate, and in a timed reaction-test answered 'Summit' to every question put to him. I could do nothing with the man.

Last patient to-day was a thin, nervous type, with pince-nez. Very pale, hands ingrained with ink, tips of the fingers flattened and calloused from typing. I put him down as a Boxing Correspondent or Twelfth Man, but he corrected me. He writes gardening notes twice weekly in a London daily, and is oppressed by a fear that he is beginning to repeat himself on Flowering Shrubs. I could find no previous instance of this particular phobia in my case-notes and was greatly interested. Apparently there is not much you can do with flowering shrubs except give long lists of those that do well in shady places and those that don't, so that, as my patient put it, 'it's a job to keep your originality and freshness, when you've been at it twenty-five years'. I mentioned pruning, but it appears that pruning is a matter of making long lists of those that flower on last year's wood and those that don't. I need time to consider his case and fell back on the old dodge of insisting that we build him up physically before tackling the mental side. 'You must get out more,' I told him. 'Three weeks at Kew will make a different man of you.'

TUESDAY. A depressing day. People think that medical men become hardened, incapable of seeing the personal tragedy behind what is to them merely another 'case'. It is not so. One feels at times so utterly inadequate.

One of those Literary Miscellany men came in to-day. Not outwardly broken down, and no sign of mental anguish in speech or manner during the preliminary general chat I always encourage, though I noticed he had the Deferred Negative pretty badly. But when it came to the point and I asked him straight out what seemed to be the trouble, he began to shake all over. Couldn't speak for a while and simply thrust a bundle of cuttings of his own work into my hands. My eye was at once caught by a num-

ber of expressions heavily ringed—'How admirable a thing it is . . .' '. . . boon companions of an idle hour', and so on. There was even an 'O fie!' 'You see?' my patient said, with tears in his eyes. 'Do what I will, these vile gentilities come me cranking in. Why, I know not.' I at once began to question him about his adolescence, and found, as I expected, that he had been a heavy reader of Charles Lamb in his formative years.

There was nothing that I or any man could do for him, and I told him so. It is the kindest thing in the long run. He took it well, only asking me quietly whether it would get worse.

'I am afraid so,' I said.

'How long have I got?' he asked.

I shrugged my shoulders. 'Eighteen months. Perhaps two years. It depends on your Editor. You might hold the thing at bay for a time by the use of antidotes.'

---

[1] 'Brooks no delay.' A contraction used by psychologists for 'The urgency of the problem brooks no delay'. Leader-writers who conclude their leaders in this way often suffer from a feeling of frustration and neglect.

'And then?'

'Woman's Hour,' I said bluntly.

I prescribed a course of Raymond Chandler, to give him a straw to cling to. But it is all quite hopeless.

WEDNESDAY. Nothing of much interest. A typical repressed Motoring Correspondent, forced by policy considerations to sublimate 'The new model has a tendency to shear the crown wheel after five hundred miles' into 'One or two minor faults which the manufacturers have in hand'. Also a publicist with delusions of grandeur, and a markedly claustrophobic contributor of 500-word detective stories to the *Evening Standard*. Pure routine.

Rather an amusing interview with a City Editor, who went into a long rigmarole about market trends and wanted to attribute his increasing languor and loss of confidence to his failure to foresee the rise in the Bank Rate some time ago. Quite by chance he let out that he had recently married a widow! I bundled him off in quick time to a Harley Street man who deals with that kind of problem.

THURSDAY. A young man called for an aptitude test. What a relief it is when the usual stream of em-

bittered, overworked or maladjusted drudges is interrupted by a fresh uncomplicated mind, wanting not consolation or a cure but simple guidance! My practice with these would-be journalists is to converse with them on general topics at first, taking careful note of any marked trick of speech or turn of phrase. Often it is possible to grade a man successfully from a single expression or even word. Thus, if he starts every third sentence with a challenging, 'Make no mistake . . .' I recommend the *Daily Express*; if he is fond of the word 'disquieting' I send him to *The Times*; and so on. The method works well, and often years pass before men I have 'placed' in this way return as regular patients.

My caller of this morning, however, betrayed no definite indications, beyond a certain liveliness of phrase which inclined me to jot down a tentative '? Guardian' on my pad. I therefore proceeded to the Headline Test. This consists, of course, of a series of brief news items, to which I ask the patient to supply the first headline that comes into his head. The test is of great value in revealing the cast of mind, and the results are almost invariably diagnostic. I began, as usual, with the classic, 'A well-dressed visitor crashed to his death in a cask of sulphuretted hydrogen at Clifton, Glos., early yesterday', expecting the normal reaction, 'Clubman in Vat Death Fall', or, 'A Tragic Mishap at Clifton', as the case might be. To my surprise he at once replied 'Acid Drop'. Similarly, to an item about a leg of lamb found on a billiard table at Bournemouth, he replied 'Potted Meat', and when I followed this up by reading a brief account of a woman of title who had been reduced to eating chest-

nuts in the New Forest he responded, without hesitation, with 'She Stoops to Conker'.

Sent him along with a note of introduction to the front-page editor of the *Evening News*.

FRIDAY. As one gains experience, it is sometimes absurdly easy to make an absolutely instantaneous, and correct, diagnosis. None the less, the feeling of satisfaction persists—and the patient, of course, is at once inspired with confidence in one's ability to help him, which is half the battle. Man rushed in this morning, purple in the face, and *gibbered* at me. Kept tapping himself on the chest and holding his hands out in front of him about eighteen inches apart in a vertical plane. Then he'd thrust his right hand almost into my eye, with the forefinger and thumb an inch apart as though holding a lump of sugar. Then he'd reverse the process, mouthing and mumbling the while in a thoroughly unorganized manner.

'The trouble with you Radio Critics——' I began.

He collapsed into a chair and regarded me with positive awe while I ran quickly through the main features of his case. 'You used to do five or six hundred words,' I suggested, 'at a time when your paper's TV man, if there was one, had at most a couple of inches. Right? Now the boot's on the other leg with a vengeance. *He* gets the top of the column——,'

'A column and a half,' he snapped. 'And half-inch heads over the two.'

'Exactly. While *you* are lucky to be left with a couple of sneering paragraphs about Saturday-Night

Theatre. So what? So you come creeping to me—as though *I* could resuscitate the sound radio you've done nothing but pick to pieces all your working life. Be off with you!'

This direct attack brought him to his senses, as I intended it should, and he began to discuss his situation more rationally. He told me he had thought of trying for some gramophone-record reviewing in the serious weeklies, to eke out. I regarded this as a policy of despair, and said so pretty sharply. I get tired of these people who will not try to move with a changing world. Why on earth doesn't the man turn himself into a nuclear fission expert, or offer himself as Space Critic to the *Mail*? The shining example of adaptability, in my experience, is the retired Brigadier who came to me shortly after the end of the war, complaining that he couldn't sleep. The root of the trouble was that acceptances of his articles on the Use of Armour in Modern Warfare had fallen off by over sixty per cent since VE Day. I told him to face the facts, and he went straight out and did a series on Tea Shops in the Home Counties. Result, he is now a household name, eating cucumber sandwiches twice-weekly on Television, and all his cakes are gâteaux. It is simply a matter of flexibility and keeping abreast of the times.

SATURDAY. Agreed to see two urgent cases at home—both women. The first had a contemptuous look and fired off two witticisms before she was well inside the door. I have learned to look for jealousy as the prime disturbing factor in female film critics, but this lady's trouble was a different kind. She has begun to dream in Technicolor, she told me; and, what is worse, her dream-pictures appear in Wide Screen, so that her nightmares are three times as frightening as before. I advised a long holiday abroad, but it appears that everywhere she wants to go has already been recommended by her paper's Travel Correspondent, and she would rather die than take that

woman's advice. This is an unusual and complicated case, which will need further consideration.

My second patient was very much younger, stylishly dressed and undeniably attractive. She had a way of looking on the bright side of everything, so that it was some time before I discovered that she had lost her husband through taking her own advice on How to Make a Success of Marriage. It was, she told me (keeping her blue eyes on mine, as I like patients to do), Rather a Shock. The brute had suddenly told

her, at breakfast, that he was tired of unfailing sympathy and understanding, brushed aside the cool hand she laid on his brow, and left without another word for Eastbourne with a tactless tennis-player. As a result, my patient had lost confidence in her own cheerful infallibility and feared relegation to the jumper-knitting section.

We had a long talk, and at the end of it I felt wonderfully soothed and relaxed. I advised divorce, and asked her to call for another consultation as soon as she was free.

SUNDAY. Read the papers and noted down a number of promising potential patients. The Reversed Persecution Mania case in the *Sunday Express* is coming along nicely. Am also expecting the dreaded Purple Patches to break out any time now in the *Observer* 'Profile' man. The *News of the World*, however, remains disappointingly normal psychologically.

Query. Can 'Atticus' be going to another man?

H. F. ELLIS

'*Do you mind if we join in? The food's terrible.*'

'Is this seat taken?'

Conference at Carnoustie?

A SHORT time ago the following advertisement appeared in the *Manchester Guardian*: 'Young man, no intelligence, shocking appearance, requires post: little work: excellent salary essential. Address BO 53 *Manchester Guardian*.'

This puzzled me. Did the advertiser really imagine that some fun-loving Manchester business man would be eager to pay out good money to an idle, ill-favoured nit-wit, simply for the sheer humour of the thing? Why did he think that readers of the *Manchester Guardian* were of a more risible type than those of any other paper? If the whole affair were nothing more than a joke, surely it was a rather expensive one? Suddenly, as I re-read the advertisement, I was struck by a very remarkable circumstance: the first letters of the first six words, reversed, could be read thus—'AS IN MY'. It was no mere coincidence. In not a single other advertisement in the personal column—and there were twenty-eight—could a similar group of letters be made to yield anything coherent. I had stumbled upon a message in a secret code.

ROY DAVIS

My first thought was that it might very well be that the sender had included the key to his code in some previous issue of the paper, and by great good fortune this proved to be the case. A rapid search of the columns for something a little out of the ordinary yielded a distinctly odd *Miscellany* item—a humorous remark made by a child—and from this I soon managed to extract a series of numbers which enabled me to arrange the letters of the advertisement in a new and breathtaking order. The figures '53' were not dealt with in the key, but I found by experiment that they must stand for the fifth letter from the end of the alphabet, and the third from the beginning. Further explanation would be tedious, but perhaps I might just emphasize the fact that every letter or its equivalent in the original, no more and no less, will be found in my translation. Here it is:

EDEN MEET RED LION CARNOUSTIE AS IN MY LAST LETTER WILL CHARGE ALL GIN PARA CAR EXPENSES CONS PARTY NO RISKS COCK GOD SAVE THE QUEEN BULGANIN

Now, the irony of it all is that this startling discovery should have been made by one who is little better than a political imbecile. I know nothing of such matters, and care less. What should I do? First, at the risk of exposing my simplicity to ridicule, let me give my interpretation of the message.

Worsted in the struggle for power, Bulganin has decided to attempt a *volte-face* and carve out a new career for himself in the British Conservative Party. He envisages some arrangement by which the holder of a safe seat could be sent to work in the coal mines, while he himself secured a hundred per cent poll in the resulting by-election. His eventual aim is a seat in the Cabinet—perhaps even the Premiership itself. He feels confident enough of the outcome to adopt a fairly dictatorial tone to Sir Anthony in the matter of expenses, but he obviously wishes to run no risk of a premature disclosure of his plans. He will land by parachute at Carnoustie on some date previously specified, and make his way to the 'Red Lion' inn.

It seems to me—and heaven knows I may well be wrong—that the first question that presents itself is this: How would the British public react to the idea of Bulganin as, say, Minister of Defence, or perhaps even as Premier? I am going to come right out into the open here and say that I believe they would be against it. What are Sir Anthony's views? As regards the greater prize we can be in no doubt, but is it not just possible (or am I talking nonsense?) that he is toying with the idea of a bold bid to introduce new and vigorous blood into his team? Would this be a good thing? I do not know. Will Sir Anthony go to Carnoustie? I cannot tell.

Now, in my heart of hearts I feel that there is really only one sensible thing for me to do: I should put the whole affair squarely before the Archbishop of Canterbury and volunteer to travel with him to Carnoustie. However, I find myself reluctant to take this course, for several reasons.

First, the 'Red Lion' is not mentioned in the A.A. handbook. No doubt it is some modest public house on the outskirts of the town. Bulganin will arrive at dusk, thus minimizing on the one hand the chances of detection, and on the other the danger of crashing on to a roof top. His business will hardly be settled in less than a full evening, and it is fairly certain that we shall all have to put up at the 'Red Lion'. Bulganin probably sleeps with a loaded revolver by his pillow, and his demand for a room to himself will no doubt be readily conceded by the others. I cannot think that the 'Red Lion' will have more than two guest rooms, if that, so it follows that the Archbishop, Sir Anthony and myself will have to make our arrangements as best we can in the second. I fully realize that this is no time to be worrying about a patched dressing-gown or a habit of falling out of bed, but naturally I should wish to make a good impression on such companions, and I doubt if I shall be able to do it.

A second difficulty is my ignorance as to the exact date of the meeting. Bulganin must have arranged this in a previous message—I seem to recall an appeal for rhinoceros horns in the *Sunday Times*—but it would take days to track down both message and key, and time is precious. My fear is that the Archbishop and I will be hanging about the tap-room of the 'Red Lion' for a week or more, singing choruses for good fellowship's sake, and perhaps getting drawn into a noisy altercation from time to time. I cannot say that I look forward to it.

On the whole, I am heartily sorry that I ever stumbled upon this message, and I am half inclined to limit my part in the affair to placing the facts before the public in this article. The thing has been wretchedly worrying, and has yielded, to me, little of interest—except perhaps the identity of the contributor of humorous child anecdotes to the *Manchester Guardian*.

T. S. WATT

No Joke!

'I MUST'—comes the fluting voice—'I positively *must* have a snowstorm!'

The enthusiasts round the window press nearer. It isn't the better kind of joke shop, being one of a line of booths on an old bomb site: I come on it, garishly lit, among sea-fern products, nylons, French paste and the like. The Joke Shop proper would be well established (1875 or thereabouts), gravely situated. On this side might be found a scientific instrument-maker's, so that from the contemplation of prisms and sextants one moves on to Live Snake; on the other, issuing from Insurance, one would pause to consider the claims of Itching Powders and Rubber Chicken.

I goggle. Long, long ago I adored an ink blob; with its tangible gloss, it seemed to me the most beautiful thing in the world. I carried it with me, since one never knew when it might be wanted, in an envelope. My ambition was to situate it on a large white tablecloth—together of course with an ink-pot fallen or straight—and to lurk under the table. Gratifying indeed would be the gasp or shriek with which at last it would be discovered. Footsteps would scurry away; then, with the field clear, I would nimbly remove bottle and blob (for often I was provided with both), and again conceal myself, this time nearer the door. I don't know that this ideal concurrence ever arrived. My Spilt Ink got scratched—quite enough, I found, to banish illusion, though still at moments I would fetch it out to admire its good side.

Ink is here; so are Beetle in Tea and Fly on Sugar. Bed Bugs are classic, the only trouble with them being that not enough people seem to notice. (But that is an after-laugh, too.) Matches won't light, cards change their spots, chewing-gum snaps at you (after my time), cobras wait to be fluted to, button-holes squirt, buns squeak, cushions—very regrettably—creak. The cheese triangle is so exactly the real thing that one may presume this to be the natural end of all cheese triangles. Boiled-egg slice also has a predeterminate look. 'Put it in the salad'—quite—'but keep an eye on it'—not so easy, particularly when the shrimps and the jam spoon need watching too. (Ah, high tea!)

Everything is lying in wait—key-rings, cups, cigarettes,—with a growl or a hop, a shudder, a bang, a mere refusal to perform some expected function; and the commoner the object, the greater the shock.

'Snowstorm!'—it's that high, agitated gentleman again, with his fluty voice attuned no doubt to the cobra—'I *won't* be put off!'

'But, Julian,' hisses his bearded companion, 'you've already had six this year.'

'This is for David's poetry reading.'

A scrum of schoolboys, who have managed to wriggle their way in, point at Stink Bomb (Grade A) and rush inside. The rest of us close up, huffed, intent on resuming our study. No bookshop or wine-store could boast a more earnest clientèle. I begin to dream of cobras in hotel bedrooms; I am swept away by the possibilities of Protruding Toe—an entry, say, in full evening dress. Toe first . . . It is a very loud, an insufferable toe.

Then there is the Genuine Walnut Shell which, when split, will reveal 'a beautiful young lady in her birthday suit, having a bath.' Several youths ahead of me seem drawn, while professing an interest in The Foolish Pen. Will it split? Did not Sir Jeffery Hudson make his fortune with Charles the First by stepping out of a pie? True, he measured only eighteen inches.

He further distinguished himself in two duels, one with a turkey-cock, the other with the man Crofts, who made the mistake of arming himself with a squirt and was shot dead for his humour.

Will the walnut split? Perhaps it's like any other walnut, and that's the catch.

The two dilettantes couldn't, with a shrug, care less. The one with a ginger beard—is it real?—is trying to urge on his companion Broken Windows. Such *éclat!* But no. There may be persons—bur-glarious or paranormal persons—for whom it would be the very thing: not for him.

Amid so much that shocks and assaults I am surprised to pick up a running appeal to bashfulness. The Lovers' Fun Card Set, 'designed for married and single,' will enable any young couple seated on a sofa to exchange cards instead of words. 'If you are too shy these cards will Y-E-L-L for you.' Here, in fact, are the adjuncts for a perfect courtship. He has made his mark with Big Chest, Monocle, or whatever it may be; a roll of Stage Money—'guaranteed to make a good impression'—will have been laid on a side-table. She, seated on the sofa, quite dazzles with her Cupid's Bow or Smoochy Lips (again the individual touch) and, of course, screen Eyelashes.

At once he catches her sympathy with a Bloody Finger. She arranges a bandage, but again and again it will fly off. Or would she be more tempted by Nail Thru Finger, or Severed Finger 'faithfully copied from a genuine original'? Then, as she feels a little

faint, he will revive her tenderly with his Shower Button Hole.

So romance ripens. No chance will be missed. One day it will be a Zip Banana, the next a Revolving Bow Tie or Extruding Tongue. His Vibrator Handshake never fails to communicate power.

When he writes to her—which he does every day—a butterfly will flit out of the unfolded paper.

One night—Cat Tail dangling from pocket—he places her hand on his chest: the commotion there is much enlivened by a Heart Palpitator, which has also served at supper for making the plates lift. A pinch of Sneeze Powder will have served its purpose (two for a kiss!); the chapter in the booklet on Magnetic Eyes will have been well studied; then comes the moment to which all this has been leading up.

He hands her a cup of tea.

Sugar?

She nods.

In goes the sugar lump; and after a while there will float to the surface a Wedding Ring. He points to it, waits . . . What girl—especially one whose lover has swallowed razor blades and performed on the Zoo-phone—could resist? Provided, of course, she takes sugar.

Meanwhile, outside the Joke Shop, the dilettantes have plumped for a Nose-drop, a Bloody Dagger, and a Snowstorm—just a teeny one; newcomers are warming to Sooty Soap and the Dehydrated Worm; I turn away to face a world grown doubly fallacious. Can this passing plum-coloured visage under a bowler hat be real—is the hat? Are stubby fingers, cane and gloves, teeth—no, that deception long ago ceased to startle—cigar—which for all I know may be pouring out Arabian Night Incense . . . Oh, I'll be lucky if I get home to collapse into a chair that will collapse under me!

G. W. STONIER

'When shall I be well enough for a complete rest?'

The Last Earl of England

LORD HAILSHAM, whom the
    Commons knew
  As Mr Quintin Hogg,
Unlike the usual Tory brew
    Gave ancient ways a jog.
      He thought that peers, when
        they succeed,
      Should be incontinently freed
        From going to the Lords.
    He even thought that, if you please,
    We ought to let them stay M.P.s.
      A notion such as this affords
A dangerous precedent, said Attlee,
And turned it all down pretty flatly.

There was some more commotion
    when
  With Socialistic hump
A certain Mr Wedgwood Benn
    Also refused the jump.
      He swore he would go further still.
      He would bring in a private bill
        To keep himself a Commoner.
    'Quid est' (his father shook his head)
    'Hoc omne fus de nihil, sed
      Non eadem sunt nomina.'
But Attlee still was non-committal—
A case, he felt, for non-acquittal.

    But leaders may expound their creed
      According to their wont.
    There is a book who runs may read,
      And several do who don't.
        In *As It Happened* Attlee said
        The House of Lords was almost
          dead,
          Deserted, dull, effete.
        But, as it happened, without flap
        And much like any other chap
          He took his vermined, ermined
          seat,
    Earl Attlee, in the House of Peers
    Amid the most tremendous cheers.
             CHRISTOPHER HOLLIS

Fragments of a Future History

The Revolt against the Consumer. 'Stigwoodism'[1] was in essence 'a revolt against the tyranny of the consumer'.[2] It should not be thought that the consumer invariably accepted his deposition without attempts at resistance. The most notable of these efforts to turn back the clock was the so-called 'Cripples Riot' at Glasgow in 1968.

The Busmen's Struggle. With the closing of the railways in the 1960s the problem of how to limit the numbers travelling by other means of transport became acute. By a succession of strikes busmen had won, first the right to carry no standing passengers (1958), secondly the right to declare empty seats 'filled' (1961), and thirdly the right to carry no passengers on the top deck. Moderate as they were, these rights were none the less questioned by the travelling public, egged on by hot-headed and intransigent consumers. During the early 1960s an increasing number of incidents occurred in which conductors were attacked and overpowered in the exercise of their duties. The gravity of the situation called for special measures. In 1961 conductors were awarded 'danger money'; in 1963 magistrates were given the power to declare any bus-queue of three or more persons 'a riotous assembly'; and in 1964 a Royal Commission, headed by Dame Melisande Custard, was instructed to inquire into the whole matter.

The Custard Report, 1967. The Custard Report pointed out that transport managements and staffs were unanimous in their view that the passenger, as such, was a tiresome anachronism. By inefficient boarding and alighting he made adherence to a fixed schedule almost impossible; by tendering incorrect fares, by demanding change and by uncertainty as to destination he aggravated the conductor's difficulties. Nevertheless, the Commission felt itself unable wholly to accept the official view that travel by bus or tram should be restricted to transport employees; there was a case, it argued, for allowing members of the general public, with genuine compassionate or health reasons for travelling, to use certain routes—in limited numbers, of course, and at the conductor's discretion.

'*The Cripples' Riot*.' Even this unworthy concession to consuming interests did not allay public discontent, which, indeed, soon boiled over. Early on the morning of February 9, 1968, Mr Hector McGorbal, the conductor of a Glasgow tram bound for Partick, noticed an unusually large crowd waiting on the kerbside at Auchenshuggle. Many simulated advanced age or painful physical infirmities; some carried crutches and other appliances, and several were dressed in deep mourning. When, as he was bound to do, McGorbal demanded certificates of right to travel, signed by a doctor or minister of religion, the leader of the demonstration, a man named Nimmo, stepped forward and felled him with his crutch. With suspicious agility the rest of the mob followed him on to the tram and overpowered the driver. A man dressed in widow's weeds seized the controls. Festooned with provocatively-worded slogans proclaiming the public right to travel and accompanied by a pipe band and a growing mob, the tram moved slowly towards the city. Other trams

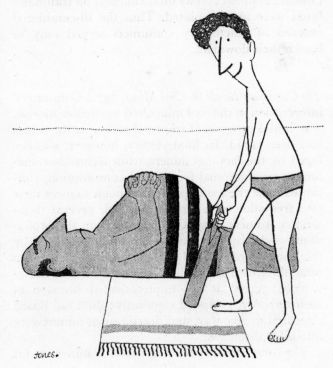

[1] *Shorter Oxford English Dictionary*, 2041 edition. 'Stigwoodism. (From F. Stigwood, English worker, -ism). A method of economic organization in which wages are paid for work of an imaginary, symbolic or economically valueless nature.'
[2] Erna Nopp, *Das Wesen des Stigwoodismus*, Tübingen, 1970.

were rammed and boarded, and by midday license reigned throughout the Glasgow transport system. Trams sped wildly to and fro, crammed with passengers, some armed and many intoxicated; several fatal accidents were caused by passengers falling from tram windows and roofs.

Withdrawal of the 'Custard Concession'. After initial hesitations the public authorities acted with commendable firmness. Troops were called in to aid the police and, after tear gas and fire-hoses had been applied, most of the trams were again running empty by the evening. The lesson was learnt; and in March, 1967, the much-abused 'Custard Concession' was withdrawn. All passengers were henceforward prohibited; to protect crews from violence, all trams and buses were armour-plated. Thus the ill-considered excesses of reactionary consumers served only to hasten their downfall.

* * *

The Consumers Invade the Coal Mines, 1972. Consumers' intervention in the coal mines had no greater success. The initial progress of stigwoodization in the mines had been rapid. Its final victory, however, was delayed by the fact that miners, while naturally reluctant to produce coal for general consumption, continued none the less to produce enough to meet their own free allowance. Greedy for fuel, several thousand consumers, drawn principally from the professional and leisured classes, were weakly allowed by the Coal Board to enrol themselves as miners and to mine their own coal. The National Union of Mineworkers, angry at this unprecedented invasion of their territory, protested vigorously; the Coal Board appeared to give way, and the consumer miners were ostensibly dismissed.

The Great Strike. A few days later a miner on his way to get coal for himself was astonished to find a clergyman, with a pick lying beside him, surreptitiously filling a bucket at the coal-face. Questioned, the man proved to be the Reverend F. St. J. Wiskin, a well-known firebrand and a shameless advocate of consumers' interests.[1] The union struck (December, 1972), and has remained on strike to this day.

The State Assumes Responsibility for Strike Pay. As the first year of the strike drew to a close it was evident that many of the miners were suffering hardship: hire-purchase instalments on cars, television sets, washing-machines, and other necessities were falling into arrears; public sympathy was stirred by the tale of a Durham miner who was forced to eat his much-prized pigeons. Despite generous assistance from Czechoslovakia and elsewhere, union funds were running low. The case for State intervention was overwhelming. The second Bevan government accordingly decided, in January 1974, that the miners' strike pay should be a charge on the Treasury.

The Stigwood National Park. Thus, not for the first time, emergency action provided a permanent solution. Few who to-day ramble through the leafy lanes of the Stigwood National Park[2] can realize that this sparkling air was once thick with coal-dust, that these green knolls were once slag-heaps, that men once toiled underground for as much as eight hours a week where now the Co-operative Youth Clubs wander at will. Had he lived to see it this transformation would have made Stigwood a proud and happy man; it is his true memorial.

JAMES ROSS

---

[1] Three years previously he had been arrested for endangering the public peace by quoting Samuel Smiles from his pulpit at Bournemouth.

[2] Formerly known as the Rhondda Valley.

'It's the weight of the medals, mam.'

HEWISON

N or M

The Court Circular recorded that Dr William Graham
had preached a sermon at Windsor.

'YOU are young, Dr William,' the equerry cried,
  'With procedural problems to grapple:
It may be all right to be Billy outside,
  But *not*, if you please, in the Chapel.'

J. B. BOOTHROYD

'I'd give a pretty penny to know what they're saying.'

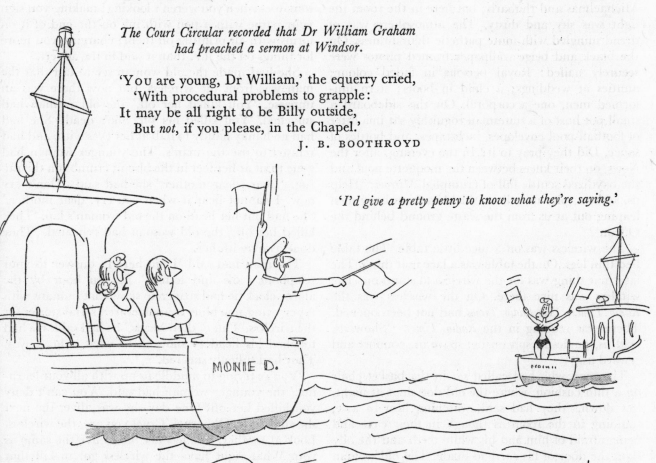

MONIE D.

Dana Fradon

This Year of Grace

Thousands of listeners telephoned the B.B.C to protest about the 'death' of one of the characters in 'The Archers'.

THE smell of dog was in the little room, and in a corner a caged bird scrabbled secretly for seed. On the hob a big black kettle stood. The window-curtains seemed to have been knitted. There was sunlight in the hard back garden, weak among the Michaelmas and rhubarb; but here in the room the light was shy and dusty. The atmosphere was of dread mingled with mute pathetic thankfulness. On the black and beige wallpaper framed photos were securely nailed: Royal persons in faded colour; aunties at weddings; a child in boots; stern uniformed men, one a corporal. On the sideboard a small pot bust of a statesman roguishly sat in a litter of football-pool envelopes, inch-tapes, and bottles of sauce. Did they pray to it? In the evening, after the News, on their knees between the moquette pouf and the oxydized scuttle full of crumpled *Mirrors*? 'Help us, save us, pity us, tell us, shield us from bogy men leaping out at us from the waste ground behind the Odeon'?

The wireless was on a nice little table. The table had thin legs. On the table was a lace mat thing. The lace mat thing was for the wireless to stand on. The wireless was nice there. On the wireless was the *Radio Times*. The *Radio Times* had not been opened. There was reading in the *Radio Times*. ('Show us, lead us, guide us, spit on us: spare us, comfort and reward us.')

The man who had called sat in the basket chair on a thin cushion, where the old dog slept at night. 'Sit down,' they had said, watching him in awe, standing in the room as though in their cave and being afraid of him and his white teeth and the oily slam the door of his car had made. The old woman crouched in her rocker, her old feet cosy on the rag rug. She looked intently at the man who had called,

without hope or understanding. She had thought he might have come about the insurance; or about Arnold being knocked down perhaps by a big lorry going to work and having to have his leg off; or the outside lav that the landlord wouldn't look at.

The younger woman's look was crafty: she did not trust the man: you did not trust people, because they were out to do you all ends up—giving you soft tomatoes when you weren't looking; making you sign your name with a pen with ink on the end of it on forms with all printing on them; charging you more for things on the H.P. than it said in the advert.

She had made the old woman see at last that the man was from the wireless, but now there was an impasse. 'You killed her off,' the old woman had snivelled. 'You killed her off. She's dead.' She had had no hanky handy to dab at her eyes with, and had refused to use the man's. The younger woman had gone to sit at her feet in the biscuit crumbs on the rag rug. 'Dear, dear mother,' she had said. 'Don't cry now. I cannot bear it when you cry, dear mother.' She had put her head on the old woman's lap. 'They killed her off,' the old woman had repeated. 'They done away with her.'

The man had said 'I am here in answer to your telephone calls and letters.' For an hour by the alarm-clock he had striven to show that humans with typewriting machines manufactured serial stories for the wireless. 'Out of their heads,' he had said. He had touched his head to show them what a head was. They had sullenly sneered.

'You're trying to muddle us up with all your learning,' the younger woman had said. 'You can't deny you killed her off. One day she was alive, the next she snuffed it. Oh, cruel. Cruel you are, the wireless. Look at mother. She has her life to live the same as you. What right have the wireless got to kill that lady? Like a friend she was to mother, like it might be me, or Mrs Harcourt up the road. You have gone

and brought our wreath back what we have paid out good money for as a tribute to that lady and how dare you? We bake them cakes on all their birthdays and cut their photos out—how dare you throw our wreath back in our face as if we was dirt? When Arnold arrives home for his tea you will cop it, for Arnold doted on that lady also. Someone has poisoned her, you are trying to hush it up.'

'Why won't they let me see the body?' whined the old woman. 'Murderers,' she said. 'A dirty pack of murderers, the wireless.'

'A figment,' the man had stammered. 'She was merely a figment, do you see? What of Little Nell? *She* had to die.'

They did not know of Little Nell.

When Arnold had come home the man had seen that there was a black diamond on his sleeve, and that was when the impasse came.

The man looked into his hat and wished he could communicate with the old woman, the younger woman, or Arnold. They did not need pity, it was too late for that. They were too hostile in their implacable grief to hear of any explanation which might rob them of it.

In the long lines of gritty streets all round them, the darkness slowly came. Dirty water sniggered into grids along the gutters, hake warmed over chip-shop ranges, yellow-faced girls stood by the bus-stop and tried to keep their mouths closed. Knobs were turned in front rooms, the great gaunt eyes of the telly-boxes stared back sightless at the fathers in the best armchairs. Dream and horror, myth and syrup, truth and dare, fear and healing balm, sweetness and death, came hushing down in an ominous blanket over the weary town, under the pointing chimneys, at the edge of the endless moorland, and the man from the wireless had nothing at all to say as they crept up close and smothered him, to save the lovely wreath.

ALEX ATKINSON

'*This is Mr Borage, our next door neighbour, and may he borrow our lawn mower?*'

Traditional English Jungle

Just now our long herbaceous border stands in prodigal disorder:
   Ambition has outrun discretion: some of it will have to go.
So we'll scrap the great autumnal daisies, let the phloxes go to blazes
   And even the chrysanthemums although they've always made a show.
But we'll keep the little Papuan poppy which provided Sackville-West with copy
   And we'll keep the sickly annuals we tried to grow ourselves from seeds.
Still the trouble's hardly worth the taking: what will fill the gaps we're making
              Is weeds.

PETER DICKINSON

'It has stopped raining.'

Nothing for Something

'INSURANCE Companies are Revolting,' said a thoughtless headline on a recent financial page. Perhaps that goes too far, but for most people they do have a certain easy repellence. It may be a growing coyness among the insurable public which prompted a recent vade-mecum for the catastrophe-prone layman, the man who habitually reverses into his own gatepost, blinds caddies with his approach shots, loses limbs, sets curtains on fire and comes home to find that the children's pony has kicked the postman's teeth in. This man is always rushing to read his insurance policy and finding that his bad luck has come at a time, at a place or in a form which excludes him from benefit, and he feels cheated and bitter.

As the book makes plain, this is nobody's fault but his own. What he doesn't realize is that insurance companies are in business for the money, not as independent programme planners in competition with the welfare state. He should put himself in the company's place, and think how far he would get if he just sat around all day dashing off cheques. It could ruin him.

Nor does he realize that however much insurance a man has, he always needs more—a point which is made indefatigably by all insurance publicity, but which he ignores until it is too late. Owing to ignorance of the English language, he thinks, for instance, that a Comprehensive Policy on his house and posses-

sions comprehends them all, and all contingencies. It only needs a chimney stack to fall through the roof and wreck the spare bedroom to show him how wrong he is. Unless the provisions of his policy specifically include falling chimney-stacks—or unless, by a happy chance, he can prove they were struck by lightning—he hasn't a leg to stand on. This means that if you want your Comprehensive Policy to be Comprehensive you must see that it comprehends everything you want comprehended. For a man of imagination, getting out a list of possibilities along these lines can be an unnerving business, involving disintegration under atomic fallout, theft of cold water cisterns or portable outbuildings, structural collapse into old mine workings and destruction by stampeding bison.

Even the standard precautions taken by every Comprehensive Policy can be a bit of a let-down sometimes. 'Damage to underground water-pipes' seems on the face of it to take care of outside plumbing hazards, but it shrewdly excludes any consequent 'flood, subsidence and landslip'. In the same way, the man sleeping soundly because he knows he need fear no financial loss from earthquakes may take to waking up regularly in the small hours on learning that this clause 'excludes damage caused by shock'—which might seem to leave the contingency virtually uncovered. With an honest face, a good circumstantial story and an assessor whose digestion is in first-class shape he may recover the value of treasury notes dropped in the fire, but he won't get so much as a compassionate grunt in the matter of incinerated 'deeds, bonds, bills, promissory notes, cheques, securities, stamp collections, medals or coins'.

For the really comprehensive policy he really wants an 'All Risks'. It costs more, but oh! the peace of mind. The only trouble is that it doesn't cover all risks. If his possessions deteriorate through the action of light, atmospheric conditions, moth, vermin or other 'gradually operating causes' he won't get a thing; nor if they suffer under war, civil war or kindred risks. Nor if he packs them in a bag and takes them out of the country. For this he wants a Traveller's Baggage Policy, which takes care of everything —except that articles of value aren't covered unless special arrangements are made. (Gold watches left in train lavatories are instanced.) However, one thing

about the All Risks stands out like a beacon; the author recommends it as absolutely reliable for 'the inveterate loser of umbrellas' . . . but remember, as he mentions more than once, the company which finds itself paying out more than it is taking in 'may decide to ask you to insure elsewhere'. That's business.

There are other small, but important and interesting points. Mirror insurance, for example, doesn't cover the frame, nor the hand-basins, Dresden ware or anything else broken by the fall: nor, very probably, the seven years' bad luck. Again, if you're insured for Personal Liability don't get the idea that you're covered for Public Liability. And remember that if you have an All Sickness Policy, and get sick, they can refuse to renew it. To be confident of renewal you want a Permanent All Sickness Policy. And in either case, reasonably enough, a company

won't insure you against any sickness you think you are likely to have. That would be absurd.

The important thing is to realize that you are not bound to construct your funkhole of standard slabs of cover as advertised. With a little thought, and an explanatory letter or two, you can insure against practically anything, whether such policies can be found lying about on the insurance broker's desk or not. This disposes of the idea that no man can achieve absolute protection against everything he can think of. He can, provided he can think of it. All he has to do is to draw up his own routine clauses covering leprosy, tight-lacing, injury from falling eagles, loss of earning power through immobilization in quicksands, etc., etc., etc., and to add at the end the most important of all—the clause insuring him against the company's finding a loophole somewhere.

J. B. BOOTHROYD

159

Quominus
Illuminatio Mea

'*As I was saying to Woodrow Wyatt. . .*'

THERE is gloom on the banks of the Isis
    Where embattled Tradition persists,
And affairs are approaching a crisis
    For the Logical Positivists.

'Only Science can furnish real knowledge,'
    Say the young philosophical dons,
'Hence it pains us to dwell in a college
    Named Trinity, Jesus or John's.'

'Since Faith's a mere fad for the feeble,'
    Cries Youth, with its head in Ayer,
'To reflect that one's patron is Keble
    Cannot fail to engender despair.'

Oh, it's hard for a free-thinking maiden
    To read Wittgenstein, Hampshire and Flew
In an ethos so stuffily laden
    With St Hilda, St Anne and St Hugh.

And consider how frightfully odd is
    The fate of a Fellow whose goal's
To establish that men are all bodies
    While inhabiting rooms at All Souls.

                   E. V. MILNER

'*This product has been carefully
packed before leaving the factory.
In the event of complaint,
please return this slip. . .*'

The Stellar System

IT SAYS here 'Go after cash, prestige, favours. Handle advertising. Use,' it adds, 'initiative'.

Author is Katina Theodossiou, and that—in her 'Day-by-Day Guide' in the monthly magazine *Prediction*—was her advice about what you ought to have done on the First of July. Presumably you are a regular reader of *Prediction*, otherwise one doesn't quite see how you are getting by, let alone away with it. So one takes it that is what you did on July 1. If you didn't you were not merely foolish in disregarding the best tipster we have—straight from the stars' beam, and by this I mean no disrespect at all to Lyndoe (may Capricorn give him a 10-1 winner), or Naylor (he has been dead right so far about everything that has happened this entire year), or David Saxby of the *Sunday Express*, who recently told Aquarius chaps (born between January 20 and February 18) that this is 'rather an emotional sort of time. It seems that people say and do needlessly harsh things'—but you were entirely out of line with about twenty million of your fellow countrymen, and, I will add here, your fellow countrywomen, who have got through this past year without undue disaster chiefly by paying proper attention to what the astrologers in the Sunday newspapers have to tell them.

Be a little bit frank and self-critical, think back, and ask yourself whether or not you did or did not, on July 1, go after cash, prestige, or favours. Admittedly there are still a score of laggards in the country who

are not yet in the advertising business, and if you happen to be one of these you evidently could not have obeyed Katina's fourth instruction. Never mind. One assumes you kept as calm as possible and waited until July 2, because you had read on and could see that this was going to be quite a day. It was, if you recall, a Saturday, and Katina Theodossiou's star-chart told that there would be 'changeable conditions to-day, especially in the morning. For pleasure,' advised Katina and a number of planets, 'attend clubs'.

Fortunately Pandit Nehru and Mr 'Billy' Wallace got their copies of *Prediction* in time, and attended clubs for pleasure. So did Marlene Dietrich; and Mrs Braddock, though she missed the exact date, did her best. People not attending clubs on that date include the Chairman of the Coal Board and Mr Khrushchev, who had been asked to attend clubs less because the porter is always in the pay of *Time* magazine, and reports on every time you take a glass of sherry and a biscuit. They slipped up there, and even a cursory look at the star shows they are going to pay for the omission—heavily.

Strictly a propos of all this is that story about when this big figure on the Beaverbrook press—I can't recall at the moment whether it was Mr Frank Owen or Mr Christiansen or some character called Gordon Keeble or words to that effect—had his worst moment of the war.

Other people had told theirs—alone with Rommel

in Tobruk, alone with Wingate in Jerusalem, alone with the land-mine in Bethnal Green—and this chap (I've already stated he was big, and I mean big) had to come up with something fairly eerie, and, by George, he did. He said that on a certain Friday night he was rung up by a certain wife of a certain Chief of Imperial General Staff. (In case, by the way, you don't believe it, this story is absolutely true.) She had met this big Beaverbrook chap at a certain party, given, it may now be revealed, by a certain party, and she wished to ask a favour of him.

The favour she wished to ask of him was could he, as a favour, get a copy of the *Sunday Express* containing the star-man's stuff—just that page would do—rushed to her husband earlier than the regular delivery time of the *Sunday Express*? Because why? Because the Chief of Imperial General Staff suddenly found himself up against a 'serious, not to say vital, absolutely urgent—you do understand what I mean—military decision'. He had, she reiterated, to *decide* something. And he couldn't, she said, and never had, made up his mind to decide anything until he had read the *Sunday Express* star-man's stuff.

After that, every time this man thought of the Army he felt a queer fear, here.

And yet the Italian newspapers have been having the impertinence to attack us for what they call an 'unethical use of the stars', which, they say, is why Mussolini went down the drain, thus counteracting the silly old theory that it was because somebody else got there firstest with the mostest men.

If you have been following your planet-men carefully during the past year you had better remember that way back in that World War II (remember the incident? Interesting while it lasted) the Admiralty hired an Austrian or someone of that kind who had been a pupil of Hitler's chief astrologer. And this man's vital job in the war effort was to tell the Admiralty what he thought Hitler's astrologer was telling Hitler, so that then we should know what the stars foretold for Hitler and make it not happen.

The Admiralty for some extraordinary reason—the whole thing is written down in a book by the Austrian, or possibly Bavarian—wanted to know what day Hitler was going to invade England on. (Probably the result of one of these inter-departmental rows—didn't want to have the fighting get to the beaches and the damned Army take the credit for whatever happened.)

So this chap—the Saxon or Prussian or whatever he was—looked up the star-chart that he thought Hitler's star-chap was looking up, and he saw that what this chap was going to tell Hitler was that on a

certain date the thing to do for pleasure was not so much attend clubs as invade an island.

Well, naturally, when the flap was over it was C-R-E-T-E and not U.K. that got the business, but it very, very definitely showed that this Rhinelander at the Admiralty was more than worth his salt. Had it been otherwise we shouldn't have ever *known*. Imagine that.

If it proves anything—and it certainly does not—it is that you, and you, and you, and I mean *you* sitting there with your mouth half open, ought to have kept your weather eye at least half open for what the big gazers and predictors in the Sunday newspapers have been up to during this year, upon which all of us look back with feelings of mingled, etc., etc.

You know as well as I do that some time ago there was a row about whether these prophets were infringing some law there is against fortune-telling. If they ever were infringing they stopped immediately the stars and a man from the Yard said it would be advantageous not to infringe. So now all they do is tell you what is going to happen to you next, depending upon when you were born. And what I have to report here is that in my opinion these Capricorns (December 21—January 19) are getting a monstrously unfair break, and have been since nearly the beginning of the year.

David Saxby (and personally I feel Dave Saxby *knows*) sets the tone when he writes of the Capricorn fraternity:

'Clear cut trends in all matters. A switch in some money interest changes your views. Plans too,

'I'm probably sentimental, doctor, but I shouldn't like to lose him.'

perhaps. Best feature of the work is the betterment in domestic arrangements and friendship matters.'

Compare this—and this sort of thing has been going on far too long—with what happens to the Aries man, and I don't mind saying that I have been an Aries man all my life, man and boy, and if it comes to that, baby: born April 12.

'Aries. March 21—April 20. The early part of the week is irritating. A number of private concerns get fouled up through other people's stupidity. By Thursday you should have sorted this out.'

Hoping against hope that Dave could have got his signals mixed, I rushed back to the daddy of them all —*Prediction*—to see could there be something nicer. What it said was:

'While some Sun-Arians will have nothing to complain of, many will feel slightly discontented—perhaps because life seems to lack sparkle and excitement. The big thing is to see that there is enough variety and interest in your life during July. You need to make a conscious effort to entertain, to go to concerts, parties, and sports meetings, and to fit in weekend trips.'

Twisting the knife, John Naylor—and I don't doubt him for a minute, I wish I could—goes on to say:

'Others in the family circle are bound to be having an eventful time.' (Hi-ya, Foster D!) 'In fact your own plans and affairs may be thrust into the background because it is necessary to entertain a relative or give them a hand with something they are doing ... With a little effort' (Naylor tells us) 'you could make the neighbours jealous.'

But just as we are getting exhilarated comes once again the warning:

'Financial prospects this month will depend very largely on what is going on in the family circle. Money may be eaten up because you have to entertain relations.'

Auntie! Auntie! Please not!

Roughly from the fall of Dien Bien Phu until whatever it is that is happening now, everyone seriously concerned has been reading the papers to find out what they should do, and immediately acting on the advice given. This fully explains everything that has, very roughly speaking, happened. It is why things are getting better. And if you find yourself a shade under the weather—like us Sun-Arians—best thing you can do is buy a Glama.

'A.P., a gentleman, writes:

'Just to let you know I have had five wins since receiving my lucky Glama—all my friends want one now.'

I believe that if Senator McCarthy and good old G for Georgi Malenkov had had a Glama—'all the mystery and magic of the Changeless Orient' (Hi-ya on 'Changeless', 'Chou-en-Lai?') 'surrounds this wonderful Talisman ... a secret symbol embodying the mysterious charms of the Ancient East, owners of this Talisman claim that Glama will bring wonderful fortune to those who have been constantly dogged by ill-luck'—they would have had a distinctly happier year. Never too late to begin. It says here 'Good week for not doing anything more unusual than customary. Watch grocers. Some interests may prove more interesting than sometimes.'

Rush this to Bulganin and Dulles.

CLAUD COCKBURN

'Aren't you supposed to be on a diet?'

'Oh come, come, Miss Levine. Dry those tears.'

167

Not as a Total Stranger

BY NOW I have run across most of the types composing the medical profession, from the highly academic to the highly alcoholic. Except one—the dedicated young doctor, a fellow who could be easily spotted by any layman with a library list.

He is generally a Scotsman or a Welshman, because Englishmen, having no quaint ways of hiding their ignorance, are never taken seriously as doctors; and everyone knows that Irish doctors aren't born but rise professionally like Venus from a sea of stout. Americans are the most dedicated of the lot, as they become dedicated very easily about anything. It is simple to understand why the young lad wandering barefoot behind the kindly, old, insanitary Kentucky physician feels that he *must* devote his whole life to medicine, particularly if he gets to hear of the old boy's income.

Dedication, except to sport, is discouraged in the English medical schools and made impossible by the English medical syllabus. The boy burning with medical ideals for five years on a schoolroom bench arrives to start work for his first M.B exam uplifted by the thought of at last joining the devoted white-clad army in their ceaseless battle against disease and human misery. He finds himself faced with a vertical board on which three weights joined by bits of string run over Meccano wheels, with instructions to demonstrate the parallelogram of forces. This is, in fact, the most difficult part of the medical course, as the weights keep flying off like a South American bolas. By the time he has recovered them several times from among his fellow-students, one of the crusty old physics demonstrators asks why he hasn't got a job as an office boy instead of wasting everyone's time in a medical school.

The dedicated student may find more satisfaction in the zoology lab, but cutting up a cockroach is a barren exercise to a youth who has seen himself doing cholecystectomies since the age of six. When he rises in the evolutionary scale at the end of his first year from dogfish, frog, and rabbit to the human frame, he may expect his ideals to be more widely appreciated. This is not so. He is taught anatomy by anatomists, physiology by physiologists, and pharmacology by pharmacologists, who regard any suggestion that this knowledge is to be used in the treatment of sick human beings as rather vulgar.

At last the dedicated young man leaves the labs and enters the hospital wards. The devoted white-clad army is now all round him, telling him to keep off the newly-polished floor, take yesterday's specimens down to the pathology department, not to use the pink cake of soap which is reserved specially for Sister, and to be a decent chap and give the house surgeon's car a shove to get it started. He will be gratified to find that human misery is everywhere, lying in bed smoking pipes while simultaneously listening to Mrs Dale's Diary on the headphones and reading the *Daily Mirror*. If he approaches the bedside in his new white coat with an air of deep professional earnestness he will certainly be taken for the hospital barber. If he comes humbly to learn the healing art from these poor stricken bodies that he might prepare himself to cure others, he will discover that the whole ward drops into a mysterious coma on his approach. The healing art is anyway severely restricted to the hours from ten to twelve and two to four, being interrupted for bedpans and lunch.

Dedicated young doctors in films are for some reason always surgeons—physicians are thought either cynical old fee-splitters or not really doctors at all because they don't dress up. I admit that surgeons exist who believe they have been placed on earth by God to save mankind, but this attitude of mind is so common in newly-elected Fellows of the Royal College of Surgeons that no one takes any notice.

Old Blood and Thunder, the man who taught me surgery, often demanded during his ward rounds why the devil some poor muddled pupil had ever decided to study the subject at all. Usually he received no reply, because a student frizzling in the glare of his personality was generally wondering exactly the same thing. But one of our class, a thin, pale man who rarely spoke, murmured one day that he 'wanted to save lives'. 'Then why,' Blood and Thunder roared, 'didn't you join the ruddy fire brigade?'

Of really dedicated students I can remember only one—a dignified balding youth who was already beginning to look like the patent-medicine advertiser's idea of a doctor. Even when cutting up his first earthworm he declared that he had heard the call; but it must have been a hearty shout, because after five years' struggle with his first examination he took a job as an insurance agent. 'Sorry and all that,' explained the Dean, throwing him out of the medical school as kindly as possible, 'but you've just got to face it. You'd simply never make a doctor.'

RICHARD GORDON

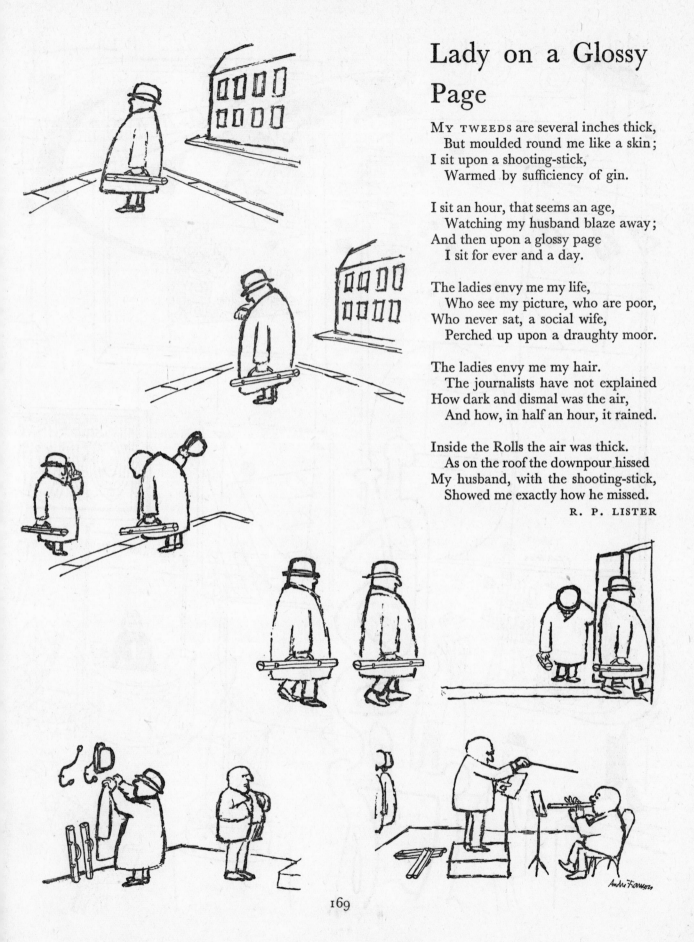

Lady on a Glossy Page

My TWEEDS are several inches thick,
    But moulded round me like a skin;
I sit upon a shooting-stick,
    Warmed by sufficiency of gin.

I sit an hour, that seems an age,
    Watching my husband blaze away;
And then upon a glossy page
    I sit for ever and a day.

The ladies envy me my life,
    Who see my picture, who are poor,
Who never sat, a social wife,
    Perched up upon a draughty moor.

The ladies envy me my hair.
    The journalists have not explained
How dark and dismal was the air,
    And how, in half an hour, it rained.

Inside the Rolls the air was thick.
    As on the roof the downpour hissed
My husband, with the shooting-stick,
    Showed me exactly how he missed.

                              R. P. LISTER

INFORMATION

ffolkes

This is Your Christmas Carol

The Studio is so small that there is scarcely room in it for the Sympathetic Understanding, Hearty Common Sense, Soothing Words, Keen Insight, Papier Mâché Sincerity and Fatherly Advice with which it is crammed. The walls drip with Love. The air is curdled with Good Deeds, and all concerned have to slop around in the Milk of Human Kindness, which is constantly sprayed into the place through a hole near the ceiling, and drained off (a bit grey) into underground tanks ready for the next time. A hidden organ plays sacred music such as 'Danny Boy', 'Bless This House' and 'My Yiddisher Momma'. Crêpe-paper decorations are festooned overhead, heavy with dust.

The auditorium is a vast arena. Men, women, children and dear little doggies, who have queued for hours in the driving sleet, sit close-packed, eating, holding hot hands, barking, kissing, sniffing, giving money to beggars, snoring, scratching, waiting for a miracle, stealing purses, or loving their neighbours. Under their feet are peanut shells, football pool coupons, frail old ladies who have dropped a glove, four thousand crumpled copies of Weekend Mail, *tea-leaves, pomegranate skins, form-books, and the small calico sachets of Sweetness and Light which are being given away at the entrance.*

To warm up the audience, Charles Dickens (with his beard shaved off, disguised as Dylan Thomas pretending to be Emlyn Williams) gives a dramatic reading from the second act of Night Must Fall.

The lights fade in the arena. Attendants with angels' wings carefully spray everybody with disinfectant. Second-hand plastic rose-petals flutter down. Somewhere a boy soprano sings 'O for the Wings of a Dove'.

Enter EDWINA LAVENGRO. *She is fetching, demure, long-suffering, with scent on her bosom, rings on her fingers, stars in her eyes. She wants us to be happy. She is in deep mourning. She is everybody's Auntie, but is not averse to a little good-natured fun after the kiddies are in bed. But she smiles bravely out at the Sea of Human Troubles that faces her, and the Sea of Human Troubles heaves in anticipation. She is followed by* TED CRAVEBLOSSOM, *a thin-lipped, hard-headed soul-searcher from the regions of the dark, satanic mills. He will stand no nonsense. There is nothing you can tell him about human frailty and the ills that flesh is heir to, because he has a corner in them. He is followed by a* PSYCHIATRIST, *a* WELFARE WORKER, *a* PROBATION OFFICER, *a* SPY *from the Wilfred Pickles Organization, a* PUBLIC HANGMAN, *some* CHOIRBOYS, *and an* OLD LADY *with a teapot who looks rather like Wilhelmina Stitch.*

They all crowd in and fight unobtrusively for the comfortable chair. They bring a smell of hymn-books and sensible cardigans. EDWINA *folds her plump, cold, soothing hands and speaks.*

EDWINA: To-night, friends, we are to consider the case of an ordinary man in the street—a humble clerk, with a wife and actual children—who has consented to lay bare his soul so that we may scrabble about in it for your enjoyment. If he can make us cry, we will be thankful: there are so few tears in the pell-mell rush of the world to-day.

A VOICE: Hear, hear!

An ATTENDANT *brings on a bucket.*

EDWINA: And if *we* can make *him* cry, so much the better. For which of us would not rather pay three pounds a year to watch some real, live, broken-hearted wretch sob his heart out once a fortnight on the Telly, than pay three-and-six to see a horror film? Which of us, I say? (*Three thousand hands go up, and a dear little paw.* TED CRAVEBLOSSOM *blows his nose. The* OLD LADY *with the teapot takes a swig of medicinal rum, and winks at a man in the orchestra.*) Very well, then. Bring on this poor little man. We have put his head in a small sack, so that you won't know who he is.

The POOR LITTLE MAN *rushes in, carrying the sack, and sits down facing the cameras. He looks peevish.*

POOR LITTLE MAN: I'm Bob Cratchit, and I don't care *who* knows it, so there!

EDWINA (*meekly*): So be it, Mr Cratchit. (*Kindly.*) Now . . . in your own words . . . what sordid predicament have you got yourself into? Open your heart, and let us revel in its seedy mysteries.

CRAVEBLOSSOM (*icily, relentlessly kind*): I think we know this poor creature's pitiful tale. Mr Cratchit, you are employed as a clerk, are you not, by one Ebenezer Scrooge?

CRATCHIT: Yes, your Honour.

Laughter. CRAVEBLOSSOM *blushes. He always wanted to be an Usher at the Old Bailey.*

CRAVEBLOSSOM: Your stipend, or weekly remuneration, is fifteen shillings, is it not?

CRATCHIT: I wish it was. It's twenty-five bob now, the more's the pity.

CRAVEBLOSSOM: You worked for Scrooge in a

171

draughty tank of an office, with no coal-scuttle of your own, and never a kind word?

CRATCHIT: I did! Those were the days! (*He sighs*).

CRAVEBLOSSOM: You struggled hard to maintain a wife and six children?

CRATCHIT: It wasn't such a struggle. Look what we used to have on Christmas Day. A goose, stuffed with sage and onions; apple sauce; mashed potatoes; gravy; a pudding, with half of a half-

'*Listen, darling—our tune.*'

quartern of brandy poured over it and ignited; apples, oranges, chestnuts; and a jug of hot gin and lemons. What *more* did we want?

CRAVEBLOSSOM: I put it to you that it *was* a struggle. It is on record that one Christmas Eve you ran all the way home from Cornhill to Camden Town!

CRATCHIT: High spirits, nothing more.

EDWINA (*rising, brushing away her tears*): But it *was* a struggle, Mr Cratchit! Your poor wife in a twice-turned gown . . . (*The audience is racked with sobs.*) No coal-scuttle in your office . . . no kind word from your employer . . . and your poor little son Tiny Tim pattering about on his little crutch, sing-

ing in his plaintive voice a song about a boy lost in the snow. . . .

Women faint. There are cries of 'We want to see Tiny Tim!' A hundred and eighteen telegrams are handed to CRAVEBLOSSOM. *He reads them out. They are from people who want to buy Tiny Tim, people who want to marry Bob Cratchit, people who have bundles of clothing for Mrs Cratchit, people who want to marry Tiny Tim, people who want a lock of Craveblossom's hair, and people who want to marry Edwina Lavengro. Attendants enter, bearing gifts that keep arriving from all parts of the country: refrigerators, once-turned gowns, oxidized coal-scuttles, geese, perambulators, crates of lemons, lame* guide-dogs, aluminium crutches, sacks of smokeless fuel, unwanted children, and a motor-car taxed and insured for six months.

SCROOGE (off, dancing with the ghost of Mrs Fezziwig): Ha, ha, ha, ha! Hilli-ho! Chirrup!

BOB CRATCHIT groans.

CRAVEBLOSSOM: I put it to you, Mr Cratchit, that your employer has made your life a misery because he is a grasping skinflint——

CRATCHIT: No!

CRAVEBLOSSOM: That you can bear it no longer, and that your problem is this: would you be justified in poisoning Mr Scrooge's gruel?

MRS CRATCHIT (rushing on with her mouth full of smoked salmon): Nonsense! That's not the point at all! When Mr Scrooge was a grasping skinflint he went his way and we went ours. But ever since he saw those ghosts we haven't been able to call our souls our own. That's what made our life a misery!

EDWINA: You poor, misguided fellow-human! We feel for you—please believe that, Mrs Cratchit. We feel deeply for you, and your husband, and Mr Scrooge, and——

VOICES: We want Tiny Tim! We want to see him suffering with a smile on his little pinched face!

EDWINA: As I was saying, Mr and Mrs Cratchit, you evidently don't understand the nature of your own misery.

The PSYCHIATRIST puts on his spectacles and takes a big book out of his brief-case.

CRATCHIT: Humbug! We understand it perfectly well! The trouble is this: since Scrooge lost his wits we've been pestered to death by his generosity. It's Christmas every day with him! He comes bouncing round every night with bottles of gin, and crystallized fruit, and sides of bacon. We have to sell half the stuff on the quiet before it goes bad. Then he's continually bringing fiddlers into the house with him, and getting up dances, and playing forfeits, and squeezing my missus in the pantry on the sly. Not content with that, he invites his odious nephew, Fred, and Fred's giggling wife, and her sisters, and the kids can't get a wink of sleep for the hullaballoo, and the neighbours keep sending solicitors' letters, and I'm too tired to get up in the morning. Then he raises my salary, and my daughters put on airs, and spend more on clothes in a month than I can earn in three. He gives me a roaring fire in my office, summer and winter, and keeps coming in to ask me conundrums out of crackers, laughing his silly head off, so that I have to stay late to get any work done at all.

EDWINA (shaking her head with a sad smile): I think you've got it wrong, you know.

CRATCHIT: Bah! Humbug!

A MEMBER OF THE PUBLIC (rushing in from Epping): I want to adopt the poor little consumptive rat that was found in a cruel trap!

AN ATTENDANT (gently): Different studio, friend.

MEMBER OF THE PUBLIC: Oh! Sorry! (He rushes out.)

CRAVEBLOSSOM (pointing accusingly at CRATCHIT): You can't deny that you have been ground down by this grasping employer, who thinks of nothing but his bank-balance. To prove it, I intend to call in. . . . (His voice breaks. He is revived by the resident MEDICAL OFFICER.) . . . I intend to call in Tiny Tim!

Pandemonium. Fire-hoses are turned on to prevent the audience from storming the stage. Teen-age girls don sweaters embroidered with the words 'Tiny, I Go For You'. Everybody cries. A man called WILFRED beats frenziedly at the main doors, calling 'Let me in! Let me in!

You can't do this to me!' He is led away, sobbing with grief and frustration. SCROOGE *seizes the opportunity to hurry in with a bunch of mistletoe, and wrestles with* EDWINA *in a corner for a good ten minutes. At last* TINY TIM *is carried on, shoulder-high, by a detachment of good, pure, flat-chested* CHORUS GIRLS. *He has grown a moustache.*

TINY TIM: Put me down, curse you!

He is cheered for an hour and a quarter. They sit him in a golden throne decorated with hearts, flowers and surgical appliances. Some fool, a bit confused, gets up and says grace. A coach-party of visiting butchers, hastily diverted from the Victoria Palace, hurries in to shake hands with him. He bites one. CHARLES DICKENS, *thoroughly delighted, wipes off his make-up and goes home to have another shot at finishing 'Bleak House'.*

CRAVEBLOSSOM (*barely able to speak with suppressed emotion*): Dear Tiny Tim! The Telly has waited for this blessed moment. It was for this moment that the Telly was originally invented! This is, as you can understand, all we needed. To see your little crutch! To hear your plaintive voice! To suffer with you as you bravely face the world! Would you mind, first of all, sitting up on your daddy's shoulder for us?

TINY TIM: Go to the devil! He's none too steady on his pins, and never has been. (*Shocked silence.* TINY TIM *lights his pipe.*) What d'you want, anyhow?

EDWINA: Ah, what an example it is to us all to see such a good, kind, noble, generous, beautiful, sweet-natured little gentleman——

TINY TIM: What are you raving about? What makes you think I'm good, kind, noble, generous, beautiful or sweet-natured, for God's sake?

EDWINA (*wide-eyed, hamming it up*): But you *must* be! You're a cripple!

TINY TIM (*furiously*): Well, God bless us, every one! That does it! get out of my way, you raddle-faced harridan, or I'll beat the living daylights out of you!

He jumps down from the throne, and lays about him with his little crutch. Sparks from his pipe set fire to the decorations. Panic spreads. EDWINA *falls face-down in the Milk of Human Kindness.* SCROOGE *grabs a* CHORUS GIRL *and sneaks off down the fire-escape, laughing heartily.* TINY TIM *fights his way out of the burning building, and the sound of his little crutch goes pattering away into the distance. There is no sign of a taxi, and his language is simply awful.*

(What befell at the Studio conference the very next morning; how it came about that Ebenezer Scrooge, Esquire, found it necessary that same night to dance upon a policeman's helmet while in the process of being taken into custody in company with a young lady not altogether unfamiliar with the theatrical profession; by what strange and unfathomable chain of circumstances it happened that Bob Cratchit retired from business to devote the rest of his life to a protracted suit for slander against the Telly; how the fire was brought under control despite all the efforts of the audience to keep it going by reason of their chagrin at the departure of Tiny Tim; how much Miss Lavengro and Mr Craveblossom made out of the night's work, and what sort of Christmas they had; these, and other unnecessarily complicated questions, which nobody in his right senses would ever dream of asking anyway, must remain unanswered until a later chapter.)

ALEX ATKINSON

INDEX OF AUTHORS AND ARTISTS

INDEX OF AUTHORS AND ARTISTS